C0-ATN-572

AFRICAN HANDBOOKS: 7

Liberia:

A Century of Survival

AFRICAN HANDBOOKS: 7

Edited by H. A. WIESCHHOFF

Committee on African Studies, University of Pennsylvania

LIBERIA:

A CENTURY OF SURVIVAL

1847-1947

By

Raymond Leslie Buell

Author of *The Native Problem in Africa*

UNIVERSITY OF PENNSYLVANIA PRESS

THE UNIVERSITY MUSEUM

Philadelphia

1947

KRAUS REPRINT CO.

New York

1969

Manufactured in the United States of America

LONDON
GEOFFREY CUMBERLEGE
OXFORD UNIVERSITY PRESS

L.C. Catalog Card Number 47-1714.

Reprinted with the permission of the original publisher
KRAUS REPRINT CO.
A U.S. Division of Kraus-Thomson Organization Limited

Printed in U.S.A.

PREFACE

I have written this little centennial volume on Liberia in the hope that the next century will be happier than the past. We are entering a tough world where the colored people will demand forcibly rights which they have hitherto not enjoyed. These rights should be granted to Liberia as elsewhere.

There are signs of a new attitude on the part of the Liberian governing class. The present Tubman administration is proving considerably more progressive than that of his predecessor, President Barclay. And the American Government is cautiously taking on new responsibilities which may bring about change. Nevertheless, unless something radical is done to narrow the gap between the governing oligarchy and the Liberian people it is not impossible that within twenty-five years fighting in Liberia will break out, as it has recently done in Java and Indo-China. Indeed, such fighting might already have broken out except for the presence of American troops in Liberia.

At the outset I should make my views clear as to racial anthropology. In my opinion, the white man awakened to the need for progress five or ten centuries earlier than the black man. This is one of the great accidents of history. Many of the problems of mankind have been due to the pressure of a higher upon a lower culture. Evil as it was, the institution of Negro slavery brought the transplanted African into intimate touch with a higher level of civilization. As the result, the American Negro today is centuries ahead of the African proper, and the American Negro has much to offer to Africa, particularly Liberia, in return. This interplay of culture, perhaps more than the negative concept of freedom, brings about the development of peoples.

But the contact between Liberia and the United States has been pretty irresponsible. Neither people makes the right use of freedom—the Liberians least of all. The Liberian oligarchy may have a sense of freedom not found in the Gold Coast, but it does not exercise it responsibly; and it is doubtful whether the past century can or should repeat itself. I am opposed to the American annexation of Liberia; but, as the last chapter of this book indicates, I believe new methods of political science should be devised to put this country on its feet and train its people for self-government.

This manuscript has been read by a large number of Negroes, Liberians and otherwise. The American Negro consultants have sympathized with the criticisms advanced against Liberia, and tend to regard conditions in that country as a reflection on the Negro as a whole. A number of Liberians, particularly officials, however, resent bitterly the criticisms and also resent delving into the past. Some of them even go so far as to accuse me of being a Firestone agent—proof of a short memory! Critical as I am of conditions in Liberia, I make them in a spirit of good will and hope of improvement.

RAYMOND LESLIE BUELL

Richmond, Massachusetts
December 17, 1945

CONTENTS

Chapter I

A NEW POLICY TOWARD LIBERIA

In 1947 Liberia will celebrate its centenary. This Negro republic, the only one in the world outside of Haiti, has maintained its independence for nearly a hundred years. Liberia has lost territory to its neighbors; but at a time when the rest of Africa has been conquered and partitioned, Liberia has remained relatively intact. Its chief achievement has been survival. This has been due to the skill of a handful of leaders, and to the fostering arm of the United States. Through visits of United States warships to Liberian ports and through more urbane gestures, the United States has posted a keep-off-the-grass sign on Liberian soil.

Liberia has an area about the size of the state of Ohio, and a population of more than one million. Lying in the tropics on the west coast of Africa, Liberia has a comparatively rich soil, most of which could be cultivated if cleared. For the most part the country is hilly. The surface soil is made up of sand, clay, and gravel. The country is lacking in limestone, however, which has to be imported for construction purposes. Liberia is rich in tropical timber, such as mahogany; but has no sawmill. Much of the timber has already been cleared by Natives, and the land is now covered with the second growth of bush. Palm trees, rich in kernels and oil, cover the hillsides and valleys outside of the forest belts.

Today rubber is the leading commercial product of the country, because of the Firestone plantations. Wild rubber is also being collected for the Rubber Development Corporation of the United States. Before the rise of Brazilian production, coffee used to be the main crop of Liberia and is still grown. In addition, piassava fiber, cocoa and coconuts grow plentifully. The country lives primarily on rice and cassava (manioc), together with eddoes and sweet potatoes. Upland rice apparently is a high-cost crop, and despite a recent law prohibiting the importation of foreign rice, except in case of emergency, rice has to be imported. This is true of other foods which should be locally produced; swamp rice is now being experimented with, producing good results.

Tropical fruits abound, such as pineapples, avocado pears, pawpaws (papaya), oranges, limes, mangoes, and breadfruit. The kola nut is grown and sold on the market. Cotton patches abound throughout the country, and there is considerable poultry and livestock. Properly organized, Liberia should become a flourishing center of tropical agriculture.

Apparently there are even greater possibilities in the mining of gold and iron. Today gold is washed out of the stream by Natives; there is no gold mine as such in the country. The iron deposits, discussed below, are considered as equal in quality to Swedish ore.

The government of Liberia is in the hands of the Americo-Liberians, a group numbering about 12,000, descended from the Negro immigrants from the United States who originally founded the country. This oligarchy attempts not only to govern itself but also the vast Native majority in the hinterland. Unlike more modern oligarchies, the Liberian Government has lacked the vitality necessary even for material development. Liberia has no hotels; no medical profession; no teachers' college or other secondary educational institutions as good as those in neighboring British colonies; no census; not even a culture of its own. It lacks adequate roads into the interior (it has no railway) and modern harbors on the coast. It has too few able men at the top; and a rate of illiteracy for the population as a whole of probably 95 per cent. Liberia has been too poor even to maintain a diplomatic mission in Washington—unlike Haiti and Ethiopia. It is a country in a comatose situation, crying out for economic, political, and cultural development. Despite its survival for nearly a hundred years, Liberia remains a sick country, perhaps the sickest part of Africa. Unless this sickness is soon cured, racial chauvinists will say, if unjustly, that the Negro everywhere is incapable of self-government.

Partly as a result of new revenues, and of the approaching centennial in 1947, the Liberian Government is now planning a number of important developments in the field of education, public health, and transportation. Moreover, it is negotiating with an American concern for a concession to exploit the Bomi Hill iron fields,[1] and also to construct a railroad from Monrovia to the border of French Guinea. It remains to be seen whether

[1] In August 1945, the Liberian Government entered into an agreement with Lansdell K. Christie of New York.

these ambitious plans will be carried out any more successfully than similar projects in the past.

As a result of World War II, the United States has taken a new interest in Liberia. Located on the hump of Africa, Liberia is actually closer in flying time to Natal (Brazil) than is Dakar. Geography has destined Liberia to be an important way-station on the sea and air routes of the world.

In World War I, Liberia followed the United States in declaring war against Germany. Monrovia, the capital, was actually shelled by a German submarine. Liberia, moreover, sent troops to France. With the advent of Hitler, Germany began to exhibit interest in Liberia; and in 1938 the American Government sent the U.S.S. *Boise* to Monrovia, in anticipation of the arrival of a German warship. When World War II broke out Liberia declared its neutrality, and did not enter the war until 1944.

With the rise of pro-Nazi Vichy in 1940, Washington feared that Dakar might fall into unfriendly hands. Meanwhile German submarines sank a number of vessels off the Liberian coast. In July 1941, Pan American Airways signed a contract with the Liberian Government giving it the right to operate in Liberia. In another agreement Pan American obtained a ten-year lease of the Liberian airport, Roberts Field. Here one of the finest land-plane fields in the world was created by the Firestone Company. Moreover an excellent seaplane base was installed at Fisherman Lake. Both these bases have played an important part in the aircraft ferry across the South Atlantic, and in the protection of rubber exports from Liberia to the United States. Moreover, after the invasion of North Africa in December 1942, President Roosevelt sent an Army-Navy Mission to Dakar under Vice Admiral Glassford as the President's personal representative with the rank of minister. This move emphasized America's strategic interest in the whole of West Africa.

Although remaining neutral, Liberia early authorized the entry of American troops into the country. In March 1942, Liberia and the United States signed an agreement giving us the right to construct military and commercial airports "and the right also to assist in the protection and defense of any part of the Republic which might be liable to attack during the present war . . ." (*see* Appendix 2). In the same agreement the American Government promised to help in the protection of Liberia, "including necessary equipment for road construction, certain monetary aids for defense purposes" and also assistance in the training of the Liberian military forces. The United States promised to withdraw "all military forces" six months after the end of the war. Although Liberia retains sovereignty over the airports, fortifications, and other defense areas established by the United States, the latter government has "exclusive jurisdiction" over such areas and over the persons living in such areas, except Liberian citizens.[2] On June 8, 1943, the United States and Liberia signed a lend-lease agreement (Executive Agreement Series 324).

Following the conclusion of the Defense Areas Agreement the United States sent Negro troops to Liberia, under Brig. General P. L. Sadler, who helped in training the Liberian forces and in the construction of roads, both for military and economic purposes. American money also replaced British currency as the legal tender of the country, as a result of an arrangement between the United States Treasury and the Government at Monrovia.

When American forces entered the country the German Government protested against what it termed a violation of Liberia's neutrality. But German "neutrality" did not prevent the Nazi radio in June 1942 from urging the Natives of Liberia to revolt. In the latter part of the year the Liberian Government requested the German diplomatic and consular officials to leave the country.

President Roosevelt stopped in Liberia on his way home from the Casablanca conference early in 1943, the first President to do so. President Barclay of Liberia returned the visit in the spring of 1943, accompanied by President-elect W. V. S. Tubman.

Finally, if belatedly, the Liberian legislature declared war against Germany and Japan on January 27, 1944; while on April 10, Consul General Walker signed the United Nations Declaration in Washington, making Liberia the thirty-fifth signatory.[3]

A further development came in the so-called Port Agreement, signed in December 1943, but published only in November 1944.[4] This agreement provides that the United States will construct a port and port works on the topographically difficult Liberia coast with lend-lease funds, believed to be at least $12,500,000. The Foreign Economic Administration allocated such funds to the Navy as the procurement agency for the port. The Navy, in consultation with Foreign Economic Administration and the

[2] *See* Appendices for the text of this and other official documents.

[3] Henry S. Villard, "Liberia's Relations with the United States," *Department of State Bulletin,* July 23, 1944.

[4] *See* Appendix 4.

Liberian Government, has planned the port, let contracts for its construction, and supervises the work. The port is being built by the Raymond Concrete Pile Company of New York City and will be completed by 1947. The agreement provides further that the port shall be administered by an American company until the loan is amortized. Although this loan is apparently non-interest bearing, it is so large (*cf.* the Finance Corporation of America loan of $2,500,000 in 1926) that it is doubtful whether Liberia can ever pay it off, particularly as annual amortization payments as well as the costs of administering the port are to come from port revenues. For that matter, it is not expected that any lend-lease loans will be repaid in cash.

That the purpose of the United States in constructing this port is more strategic than economic is shown by Article 7 of the Agreement, which grants the United States the "right to establish, use, maintain, improve, supplement, guard and control" at American expense "such naval, air and military facilities and installations at the site of the port, and in the general vicinity thereof," as may be desired by the United States "for the protection of the strategic interests" of the United States "in the South Atlantic." Although the Defense Areas Agreement of March 1942 provided for the withdrawal of American forces from Liberia at the end of the war, this port Agreement would appear to authorize the indefinite maintenance in Liberia of American forces after the war, even if confined to "military facilities" in the general vicinity of the port. With the defeat of Japan in the summer of 1945, about 1,200 American troops remained in Liberia.

It is understood that for the present the American Navy intends to install in the Liberian port only a submarine base; but that the port will be so constructed that it can be immediately converted into a major naval base in the event of World War III. Such an American base in Liberia would be in a position to neutralize an unfriendly Dakar, Freetown, or Takoradi.

In theory the American base in Liberia could be converted later into a United Nations base. But at present the pressures of world politics are not running in the direction of a United Nations solution, but rather of Big Three imperialism. Exclusive demands by Russia on Poland are being matched by the demand for exclusive American bases stretching from Liberia to the Philippines. Regardless of whether Big Three imperialism ends in World War III, the United States, through the proposed Liberian port, now has a permanent toehold in Africa.

The Liberian offer to us, first made in 1908 for a "naval coaling station," has finally been accepted.

The United States took further steps with respect to Liberia in November 1944. The FEA then dispatched to Liberia an economic mission, consisting of about six experts, headed by Earl Parker Hanson, and ranging from a civil engineer to an expert on dried fish. Its purpose is to assist Liberia "to increase its production of . . . strategic materials . . ." but its powers in this respect do not seem to be defined. Soon after its arrival, the Hanson mission became involved in a serious controversy with the Liberian Government, finally solved with the assistance of officials from Washington. The mission planned to stay in Liberia about two years.

In 1944 the Public Health Service of the Federal Security Agency dispatched a public health mission to Liberia, consisting of eleven Negro physicians, engineers, entomologists, and nurses, headed by Senior Surgeon John B. West. Formerly health officer for Harlem, Dr. West for a time served with American troops in Liberia during World War II. This mission plans to stay about five years in Liberia, to develop a health and sanitation program, to protect Allied troops there against disease, and to prevent the transmission of such disease to the United States. The cost of the mission, according to reports, will be about $350,000 to be borne by the United States, except for some $38,000 appropriated by Liberia. In addition, the Division of Cultural Relations of the State Department, which is already assisting an educational program in Liberia (page 17), contributed to the Public Health mission a few thousand dollars to improve Liberian nursing education. A mission from the United States Geological Survey in 1944 returned from Liberia, where it made a survey of the iron ore resources of the country. The United States Department of Agriculture, moreover, lent an expert to the Liberian Government at the latter's expense, to assist in a program of improved agricultural methods and better land cultivation. Finally, an educational and agricultural mission, representing the missionary societies of North America, Ireland, and Great Britain, in 1944 made a survey of such problems in various parts of West Africa, including Liberia.

Such developments represent a new American policy toward Liberia. Whether they will be really effective in curing the sickness of Liberia, as well as protecting our own interests, can be determined only after a survey of the problems and history of the Liberian Republic.

Chapter II

WHAT IS WRONG WITH LIBERIA?

Although the constitution of Liberia is modeled on that of the United States, Liberia cannot be called a democracy. The descendants of the 20,000 original Negro immigrants from America, now numbering about 12,000, keep firmly in their hands the government of the country, embracing more than one million people. In theory the governing class in Liberia welcomes Negro immigration, but in fact it is doubtful whether the Americo-Liberians would welcome real competition from the American Negro. In 1865 about 300 Negroes did enter Liberia from the British West Indies (the family of ex-President Barclay came from this group). Within more recent years Marcus Garvey and Senator Bilbo have talked about a back-to-Africa movement. But the Negro, whether from other parts of Africa or from America, shows no more disposition to go to Liberia, despite its freedom, than the American Jew shows toward Palestine. Today the Americo-Liberians are not even reproducing themselves.

Nevertheless the Americo-Liberians struggle to maintain the American tradition which their fathers brought to Africa a century ago, or at least what they thought was the American tradition. They built replicas of Southern mansions, and put their money into houses, few of which are finished. The money not expended this way is frequently deposited in foreign banks. Their "freedom" takes the form of imitating the old Southern aristocracy. It is fashionable on Sunday and on state occasions to turn out in high hats, canes, and long-tailed coats. Although the Americo-Liberians are great churchgoers, many are sexually promiscuous and have children by numerous concubines. Americo-Liberians disdain manual labor. Officials walk down the streets of Monrovia followed by small boys carrying their briefcases.

Despite an emphasis on "classical education," Liberia has failed to produce the intellectual élite found in Haiti. Moreover it has produced no leader having the outstanding qualities of the late James Aggrey of the Gold Coast, or the late Felix

Eboué, Negro Governor General of French Equatorial Africa.[1] Born in French Guiana, Eboué had a deep understanding of the need for respecting and developing Native institutions and customs in Africa.

Every Americo-Liberian strives to get on the government payroll, and usually he succeeds. About 1,000 officials are paid tiny stipends every year, most being Americo-Liberians. Few educated Americo-Liberians have any other outlet except to practise law, besieging foreigners with petty suits. Few of them have the opportunity or desire to embark upon economic enterprise of their own. Lacking an independent means of existence, they cannot oppose the government in power.

This government is ostensibly based on the principle of separation of powers. There is an elective legislature, an elected president, and an appointed supreme court. In fact, all three branches of government are controlled by a small oligarchy. The franchise is limited to individual property owners. For the most part, voters are confined to the Americo-Liberians living in the coastal towns.

Except for an interlude between 1871 and 1877, the government of the country has been in the hands of the same party, the True Whigs. From time to time opposition groups have sprung up, such as the People's Party in 1923 and the Democratic Party in 1943, but none has had a chance because a free and fair election is virtually unknown in Liberia's history. Thus, in 1927 President Charles D. B. King, who held office for ten years, claimed to have polled 243,000 votes although there were only 15,000 qualified voters in the country. President King resigned in 1930 as a result of the forced-labor scandal. He tried to stage a comeback in 1935 by organizing the Unit Whig party. Although this effort failed, and Mr. King has gone into retirement, the governing group in Liberia today is substantially the same as that involved in the slavery scandals of the Thirties. President Tubman was the "legal adviser" of Vice-President Allen N. Yancy, one of the leading slavers, and supported King in the 1935 election. Mr. C. L. Simpson, the present Vice-President, was also involved in the slavery scandals.

Of West Indian stock, President Edwin Barclay proved to be

[1] Eboué's "Memorandum on Colonial Administration" and his "General Circular on Native Policy," an English translation of which is published in *Free France,* Special Issue, No. 2, September 1944, deserves to rank with Lord Lugard's *The Dual Mandate in British Tropical Africa* (1922) as a statement of the merits of indirect rule.

the most dictatorial of all Liberian presidents. He became Acting President following King's resignation, and then was elected in 1931 for a four-year term over Thomas J. Faulkner, who had led the anti-slavery movement within Liberia but was counted out by traditional methods. At Barclay's request the Liberian legislature enacted a sedition law of 1933 (still on the statute books) which penalizes any criticism of the president or the government's Native policy with imprisonment of from three to seven months and confiscation of property. The same penalty is imposed upon anyone providing information to a foreign government on affairs of domestic concern. At the same time, the President secured the adoption of a constitutional amendment extending the life of his office from four to eight years. Barclay had the reputation of being a racial nationalist. He opposed the employment of white men in the country if an American Negro or Liberian could, in his opinion, do the job. He also secured the adoption of a constitutional amendment requiring twenty-five years' residence before one is eligible for the presidency, a provision apparently directed against American Negro troops who might decide to remain in the country after the war. Toward the end of his term, which expired in 1943, Barclay made a speech warning Liberia of the fate of the Central American countries dominated by the United Fruit Company. As the next section will show, President Barclay skilfully played the United States against the League of Nations. When he retired in 1943 he virtually selected Mr. W. V. S. Tubman, formerly Supreme Court Justice, as his successor. Mr. Tubman was opposed in the election of May 1943 by Mr. James F. Cooper, former Secretary of the Interior, who organized the so-called Democratic Party. Mr. Cooper's followers asked the government in the interest of fair play to appoint one judge and one clerk from the Democratic Party at each voting booth. The government declined to do so, continuing the Whig monopoly.

On May 7, 1943, Mr. Cooper's paper, the *Weekly Mirror*, wrote: ". . . the voting on Tuesday May 4, 1943 was the most partial, the most unfair, the most brazenly corrupt and domineering in the long shady record of the True Whig Party and in the history of the Republic." It cited the case of a dressed-up monkey taken to the polls in Monrovia to vote. "One small precinct of two dozen dwelling houses, more or less, in the Territory of Marshall, with a population in the whole territory of less than 1,000, counting men, women and children, including all domestic animals, polled 5,100 for the Whigs and 7 for the Democrats."

Curiously enough, the Americo-Liberian opposition to the Whig oligarchy has never revolted, despite threats to do so in 1923. In fact the number of able leaders in Liberia is so small that even if the opposition did win an election, the new president could do little more than reshuffle the existing cabinet. Today President Tubman has one ex-Unit Whig member in his Cabinet and another as an Under-Secretary. A few Americo-Liberians privately favor the supervision of elections in Liberia by the United States. As our experience with such a task in Nicaragua and other countries shows, this is a thankless undertaking. Nevertheless such a solution might be considered by the United States if we are going to take a more responsible attitude toward Liberia in the future.

The political system of Liberia has been marked not only by unfair elections but in the past by inefficient, arbitrary, and corrupt government. In probably the most sweeping indictment of any political system in the world, a United States representative in October 1933 summarized the situation in Liberia as follows:

> Waste of public funds in the maintenance of over-staffed or unnecessary institutions and bureaux; failure of the Department of Justice to enforce payment of delinquent taxes; failure of the Department of Justice to prosecute Liberian officials for embezzlement or diversion of public funds and Government supplies, or to take action against them under their bonds; failure of the Liberian Government to enforce the payment into the Treasury of Consular and other fees; payments of funds due soldiers of the Frontier Force, whose money was collected by Liberian politicians and their friends; failure to institute reforms and economies repeatedly recommended by the Financial Adviser.
>
> On the other hand, the Liberian Government has done practically nothing to foster or encourage commerce, or to open the hinterland to trade, a "law" on the subject passed in 1930 to the contrary notwithstanding. No progress in the uplift of the native Liberian peoples has been seriously attempted by the Liberian Government, nor have the taxes collected from the natives been spent for their benefit.[2]

Despite the presence of foreign advisers in the country since 1912, and despite the recurrent protest of the State Department, the financial accounts of the Government remain unsatisfactory. In 1938 President Barclay said in his annual message that "the accounting system of the Treasury has shown grave fundamental defects." In 1941 the American Financial Adviser declared,

[2] *Liberia,* Department of State, 1933, p. 36.

"The general accounts of the government are not in good shape and are in serious need of overhauling. For instance, there is no adequate record of the floating debt, capital investments and depreciation on plants and structures and outstanding obligations incurred by the issue of certificates of indebtedness to soldiers. . . ." The American Loan officials can verify whether a proposed expenditure has been authorized by the budget, but they lack the authority to see that the sum appropriated is actually expended for the purpose authorized. Nor do they have the powers of the receivership existing between 1912 and 1926.

Liberia's most important internal problem is the relationship of more than a million Native tribesmen to the Americo-Liberian minority. About 50,000 Natives have become "civilized" in the sense that they have gone several years to a mission or government school. The remaining Natives live under tribal conditions. Dr. George W. Harley, a medical missionary at Ganta, Liberia, says with respect to the Mano people, "Except for the suppression of war, slavery, human sacrifice and similar evils, and the assumption of political control by the Liberian government, the culture of these people remains today essentially unchanged." [3] This statement no doubt applies to most of the other tribes.

More than twenty Native tribes are found in Liberia, divided into three main ethnological groups: the Kru, the Mandingo, and the Gola. Living on the coast, the Kru are boatsmen and fishermen; they serve as deck hands and cargo workers for vessels visiting Liberian ports. The Bassa and the Grebo are related to the Kru. The Mandingo (as well as the Vai) are Mohammedans. The Vai tribe developed its own written language, one of the few such in Africa.

Liberian Natives live in small villages, making a living in agriculture. They are ruled by chiefs under a highly developed system of Native law and custom in which secret societies, now outlawed, play an important role.

Although disapproving of many religious practices of Liberian Natives, the late Dr. James L. Sibley wrote in 1926, "Altogether the native people possess many fine qualities, both physically and mentally, and undoubtedly spiritually, and constitute a great asset to the country."

In addition to governing themselves, the Americo-Liberians have tried to govern these Native tribes. When Liberia was

[3] *Native African Medicine, With Special Reference to its Practice in the Mano Tribe of Liberia* (1941), p. 6.

first established in the 1820's, Governor Ashmun and Captain Stockton made treaties with Native chiefs purchasing land for the settlers.[4]

Nevertheless a series of wars has taken place between the Liberians and the Native tribes, the latest of which was the Kru uprising of 1932. With the periodic help of American warships, and American army officers commanding the Liberian Frontier Force, the Government has succeeded in putting down Native revolts. But as the Liberian tribes become educated, they will protest more and more against abuse. Today the Americo-Liberian governing class, living in a string of coastal towns, would certainly be in a constant state of insecurity except for the overshadowing arm of the United States.

The United States and other powers have made repeated protests, reviewed in more detail later, against Liberia's abuse of the Native population; and the Liberian Government has made gestures at reform, as in 1917, 1921, and 1931. Nevertheless the underlying conditions remain unchanged. The International Commission of Inquiry in 1930 declared:

> Intimidation has apparently been and is the keyword of the Government's native policy.
>
> Not only have the native village classes been intimidated and terrorized by a display of force, cruelty and suppression, but the chiefs themselves, men whom the people not so many years ago looked up to . . . have been so systematically humiliated, degraded and robbed of their power that now they are mere go-betweens, paid by the Government to coerce and rob the people.[5]

Largely as a result of the League of Nations' reconstruction effort of 1931 to 1933, Liberia again reformed its Native policy. The five districts into which the hinterland had been divided were reduced to three provinces: the eastern, central, and western. The county superintendents who administer the areas inhabited by the Americo-Liberians on the seaboard were given certain authority over the commissioners in the provinces. Despite this latest reform, unofficial writers who lived in Liberia wrote as late as 1943:

[4] The treaties procuring land surrounding Grand Cape Mount in 1826 contained a clause to the effect that the colonists should never resell the land to any foreign subject or government. E. J. Yancy, *Historical Lights of Liberia's Yesterday and Today* (1934), p. 36.

[5] League of Nations, *Report of the International Commission of Enquiry into the Existence of Slavery and Forced Labour in the Republic of Liberia,* C658, M272, VI (1930), 86.

> Natives unable to pay fines assessed by rural magistrates are being held in pawn and made to labor long hours, without pay, until the often unjust penalties are paid. There are other natives who have been held as pawns for twenty years for having committed misdemeanors which would draw a suspended sentence of thirty days in this country.
>
> For slavery, whatever may be the pious phrases in the Liberian Constitution, is the law in practice in Liberia—the law which supports Supreme Court Justice W. V. S. Tubman, partner and attorney for the slavers [since elected President].[6]

There are innumerable cases where Liberian commissioners and Native chiefs, possibly in collusion with each other, arbitrarily seize the crops of Natives or impose arbitrary fines and forced-labor exactions on villages, causing frequent migrations. President Tubman tried to stop such practices by requiring that when an official imposes a fine, it should be paid not to him but to the nearest revenue office. He gave an instance where to liquidate a $10 fine, tribesmen had been obliged to pay their chiefs a total of from $80 to $100.

The writers quoted above, who are obviously sympathetic to the Natives, state that the tribes hate their Negro rulers "in a sullen, restless fury which may assert itself in this period of the Second World War with all the sudden fury of an African storm." "The Liberian government is simply the cancer on the body of that unfortunate nation; the Buzzi, Bassa and Vai are the staunch heart which cannot be stopped by brutality and extortion." One reason why the tribes have not revolted during World War II may have been the presence of American troops.

Going against the trend in British and French colonies to strengthen the traditional authority of chiefs, one of Liberia's reforms has been to have chiefs elected. In an address to the Liberian legislature in 1937, President Barclay admitted the plan did not work:

> This, in some sections is demonstrably true and would be seen in the inability of chiefs to secure labour to work on the public roads or for other purposes where payment is made. In two instances this was graphically brought to my notice. In the Todee Chiefdom, no roads could be built nor could the government taxes be fully collected for over a period of years. Paramount Chief after Paramount Chief had been deposed and others elected with no change in conditions. I made a visit to this chiefdom with a view to investigating the cause. The results of this investigation clearly demonstrated that these conditions

[6] Arthur I. Hayman and Harold Preece, *Lighting Up Liberia* (1943), p. 52.

grew out of the fact that the population felt themselves subject to a particular house to which they had paid allegiance for centuries. One witness said frankly that unless the paramount chieftancy was restored to that house the government would find that there would be only perfunctory obedience to its orders, since the majority of the tribe would continue to take up an attitude of passive resistance to the orders of any chief who did not belong to the ruling house.

In my conversation with some of the chiefs they professed themselves to be perplexed on this question of elections. Many of them think it an unmitigated evil making for the destruction of the moral fibre of the tribe and bringing forward men for public office whose only qualification is either their wealth or their demagogic capacity for misleading and inciting the masses.

Although President Barclay did not say so, there is a Native democracy in Africa revolving around the hereditary chief.[7] And when either a Negro or white aristocracy wedded to the West attempts to upset Native concepts rather than encourage their gradual evolution, trouble usually results.

Indeed, the future of Liberia will depend upon whether political power is gradually transferred from the decadent Americo-Liberian minority to the vigorous Native tribes, constituting the overwhelming majority. Liberians and others point out that assimilation between the two groups through intermarriage is already taking place. Certainly the gulf between the two groups in Liberia is less than that between the Creole of the neighboring colony of Sierra Leone—also founded as a home for freed slaves—and the Natives of that colony. There are a few instances also in Liberia where Natives have acquired prominent government positions; thus two members of the Supreme Court are Greboes.

Nevertheless the vast Native majority in Liberia has no right to participate in elections for the presidency or the Liberian legislature, which is confined to representatives from the coastal counties. This problem of giving tribal organizations the right to be represented in colonial legislatures, along with the educated Native, is a difficult one. But the British are trying to solve it. For example, in the Gold Coast the legislative council established in 1925 made provision for the election of the six provincial African members by the councils of head chiefs.[8]

[7] A. A. Nwafor Orizu, *Without Bitterness: Western Nations in Post-War Africa* (1944), Section IV.

[8] R. L. Buell, *The Native Problem in Africa* (1928), I, 837; Lord Hailey, *An African Survey* (1938), p. 172. Another suggestion is that a Native assembly of tribal leaders be established in Liberia. Sydney De La Rue, *The Land of the Pepper Bird* (1930), p. 223. See the new Nigerian constitution mentioned on p. 64.

Certainly the Americo-Liberians should find some similar means of giving the aboriginal population fair representation in the legislature. In his annual message of November 1, 1944, President Tubman recommended a constitutional amendment providing for tribesmen of the provinces to be represented in the national legislature. Early in 1945 the legislature adopted the amendment by joint resolution granting one representative to each of the three provinces and providing for their election by the exercise of suffrage by all Natives twenty-one years of age and over who are owners of a hut on which they pay the hut tax. The amendment was approved by the electorate at a call election on May 1, 1945 and it is expected that the new legislators will be chosen in time to take their seats when the legislature convenes in October 1945. (*African Transcripts* No. 5, Sept. 1945, pp. 143–45.)

If the Natives of the Liberia hinterland are to have the opportunities equal to those in adjoining British and French colonies, the administration of the hinterland must be improved. This is difficult in view of the present lack of central control. Until recently, at least, Liberia lacked a telephone, telegraph, and road system linking up the provinces to the capital. As a result the Native commissioner has been virtually a law unto himself. So long as the Natives have no security and feel unable to get justice either from the tribal or Liberian courts, they have no incentive to work beyond what is needed to live. This helps to explain why Liberia has to import rice.

The improvement of Native administration depends in the first instance on the construction of a road and communications system, already started by American troops. In addition, the Natives need new opportunities to develop small farms. Governor Ashmun had the dream of Liberia becoming a nation of small, independent producers. But largely because of the defects in the Liberian Government, this development has not taken place as much as in the Gold Coast and Sierra Leone. The Natives should be encouraged to grow palm kernels, kola nuts, coffee, and other tropical products; they should be given agricultural instruction; and they should be aided in marketing their produce through the type of coöperatives found in numerous African colonies.[9] They should be protected against arbitrary seizure, excessive taxes and onerous labor demands.

The greatest need for both the Americo-Liberian minority and the Native majority is a better system of education. American

[9] Lord Hailey, *op. cit.*, Chapter XXI.

missionary societies have developed most of the educational work in Liberia, whether among the Americo-Liberians or the Natives in the bush. American missionary and philanthropic organizations pour into Liberia about one-quarter of a million dollars a year, which on the average is about ten times what the Government itself appropriated for education before World War II.[10] But the type of education has not produced real leadership, at least in adequate numbers, nor has it developed an independent and indigenous church among the Native peoples such as has come into existence in China, India, and Japan and in some other parts of Africa. The denominational churches which have grown up among the Americo-Liberians have inadequate leadership. There are several institutes of "higher" education in Monrovia and elsewhere competing against each other and giving a rather poor high school education. There is lack of coördination among the missionary schools, which do not produce well-trained clergymen, let alone teachers. There is an over-emphasis on evangelism rather than on a well-rounded life. The American missionary boards agree that the results of their efforts in Liberia are less successful than in any other field.

The Liberian Government attempts to maintain its own institution, Liberia College, on a budget which during the '20s and '30s ranged from $25,000 to $30,000 a year. No Liberian educational institution has any laboratories, library, or scientific equipment.[11] The late Dr. James L. Sibley, educational adviser to the Liberian Government, wrote:

> From the standpoint of future leaders, very little can be expected of a system where there are about nine thousand children enrolled in all schools, with less than sixty in high school grades and less than twenty in college courses! . . . Liberia, more than possibly any other African group today stands in need of trained leaders to guide the country through this critical period of development. One almost marvels at the way in which this country has succeeded in maintaining its existence when one considers the lack of educational facilities in the country, and the relatively small number of leaders who have had even so much as a high school education.[12]

Since 1926 two educational improvements have been made. Under the leadership of the Phelps Stokes Fund, the Booker

[10] Henry Litchfield West, *The Liberian Crisis* (1933), a pamphlet.

[11] James L. Sibley, *Education and Missions in Liberia* (mimeographed, n. d.), makes such a statement as to Liberia College as of 1926. I understand this is still true. For the historic vicissitudes of Liberia College, see G. W. Allen, *The Trustees of Donations for Education in Liberia* (1923).

[12] *Ibid.*, pp. 70, 112.

Washington Agricultural and Industrial Institute has been created at Kakata to give instruction in agriculture and trades. Its principal is Dr. R. L. Embree. It has a staff of about fourteen teachers, including several Negro Americans, and an enrollment of about 130 boys all of whom are boarders. It operates on a budget of about $17,000 a year. Classes go through the eighth grade, and daily instruction is divided between academic subjects and actual work in agriculture and various trades. In 1944 the Division of Cultural Coöperation of the U. S. State Department made a grant-in-aid to the Phelps Stokes Fund so as to establish a mechanics training center at the Kakata Institute, and a public health center for training visiting nurses as well as agricultural demonstration stations.

The second development is that during the past year the Liberian Government has granted scholarships to six Liberian students to study at Howard University in Washington, D. C. These students appear to be doing well, and make a good impression. Lacking the means to establish a first-class institution of higher learning, Liberia in theory could profitably send its students to nearby institutions, such as Achimota in the Gold Coast, and other similar institutions. A few years ago some Liberians were sent to the Gold Coast for study; but the experiment was not continued because of what the Liberians call "the colonial complex" dominating education in the British colonies. They feel that they get better education in a spirit of freedom in the United States, where a total of about forty African students altogether are now enrolled. Here is one field where American funds could probably be better employed than in attempting to build up Liberian secondary education under existing political conditions. The number of Liberians sent to the United States to study should be increased.

Despite these developments, Liberian education, some critics insist, has lost ground on the whole during the past twenty years. If it is to develop the leadership needed to maintain its independence in the future, Liberia must have better instruction and equipment.

The Natives in the hinterland need better education, even more than the Americo-Liberian minority along the coast. Today about thirteen aboriginal children attend school to one Americo-Liberian. But many Native children never see a school. Two-thirds of those who get any education attend mission schools. While better than nothing, much of this education does little more than give a smattering of English to the Native;

it does not fit him to play a responsible part in the community. If anything it tends to uproot him from it. In a striking document, *Mass Education in African Society* (Great Britain, Colonial No. 186, p. 18), an advisory committee on education for the British Colonial Office recently wrote:

> It should be possible . . . to aim in two to three years at getting all children into school, all illiterate adults below a fixed age into reading and writing classes, all the households working at certain prescribed health and agricultural improvements, a general stimulation of local political interests and activity and increased recreational facilities of many kinds. . . .
>
> But it will be useless merely to turn out numbers of young carpenters, masons, mechanics, tailors or even farmers, with nothing but technical training in these formative adolescent years. These young technicians and farmers will have to live in a society which is facing certain major problems. . . . China has found in training boys for her industrial cooperatives that they must be given some literary instruction, some physical training, some elementary teaching in civics and economics if they are to be useful citizens as well as effective technicians.

The radio and the film—particularly the remarkable educational films recently designed by Walt Disney for illiterate peoples—should have a great influence in Africa.

In view of its origin—a home for the emancipated Negro—Liberia should have one of the most advanced educational systems in the whole of Africa. Today it has one of the worst. And in view of the incapacity of the Government, the lack of able teachers, if not the dearth of postwar revenues, it is difficult to see how Liberia can get such an educational program without some new form of outside aid. This need not be necessarily financial. Now that revenue is flourishing, Liberia should be able to increase its educational appropriations. Moreover such appropriations need to be administered with scrupulous honesty. (The story is told how the late president of Liberia College used funds appropriated for the college to send his daughters to be educated in Italy.) The Loan Agreement as amended in 1944 in fact obligates the Liberian Government to use one-third of its "excess" revenues (once the floating debt is completely paid) "to the extension of the educational and sanitation facilities of the Republic." Outside aid should take the form of teachers and educational authorities, backed by the moral support of the United States Government. Just as Liberia profited from an infusion of Firestone capital and initiative, so will it profit from the infusion of educational personnel and ideas from the United States and elsewhere. Liberia ought to have a ten-year program in which to wipe out illiteracy and to create a community type of education in which the student learns to become a more useful and happy member of the community in which he lives.

It seems only a matter of time when the preponderance of the "civilized Natives" over the Americo-Liberians will become overwhelming. Once awakened to western ideas of democracy and freedom, the educated Natives will demand the right to participate in the government, believing that eventually the Americo-Liberian minority must lose its control. Sooner or later a struggle for power between the two groups will take place. The process of assimilation now going on and the right kind of education may cushion this clash. But whether the struggle becomes violent or whether the transition of power to the Natives is gradual, depends on the wisdom of the present governing class and of the United States.

Undoubtedly some members of the Americo-Liberian oligarchy do not wish to open up and develop the hinterland because they fear an increase in the power of the Native tribes. Undoubtedly they hope that the United States, more firmly anchored than ever in Liberia on account of the new port, will continue to assist in forcibly repressing Native revolts. But certainly the American people would not stand for such a policy if they really knew conditions in Liberia; and the most enlightened Americo-Liberians also know that a repressive policy can end only in suicide.

It is possible to be too severe in passing judgment on Liberia. The abuses of government in that republic can be duplicated and possibly exceeded in other independent countries, particularly in the semi-tropical areas. Moreover, the Americo-Liberian oligarchy has never been guilty of the organized and continuous atrocities found in the totalitarian countries of Europe. Nevertheless it is doubtful whether the outside world will long tolerate the present situation in Liberia. As the next section will show, the United States is in large part responsible for the present situation in Liberia. Whatever the legal relationship between this country and Liberia is, the outside world will hold us to this responsibility. Whether the situation in Liberia will be changed, and how, depends largely on American policy.

Chapter III

A CENTURY OF INDEPENDENCE

Liberia owes its birth to the joint efforts of the American Government and certain American philanthropic organizations, chief of which was the American Colonization Society created in 1816 to settle freed slaves on the West African Coast. At that time freed slaves were not wanted in the United States out of fear that they would increase the agitation for emancipation.

The slave trade having already become illegal, Congress passed an act in 1819 instructing the American Navy to seize any American vessels engaged in the slave trade, and instructing the President to return all Negroes thus seized to Africa. During this period American naval vessels cruised off the west coast of Africa looking for slavers. The Negro slaves thus seized on the high seas and the freed slaves in America were the two sources from which the Liberian Republic emerged.

Congress, in the act of 1819, authorized the President to appoint agents to receive the seized slaves in Africa, and appropriated $100,000 for the general purpose of the law. President Monroe [1] ordered a naval vessel and two American agents to go to Africa, taking with them tools and other implements to get the ex-slaves established. These agents were instructed to select "the most suitable place on the coast of Africa" to which the captured slaves should be delivered, with an "express injunction," according to Monroe's message of December 17, 1819, "to exercise no power founded on the principle of colonization" or other power than that of performing "the benevolent offices . . . by the permission and sanction of the existing government under which they may establish themselves." In other words, President Monroe seemed to feel that these captured slaves, taken on the high seas by American naval vessels, could be put ashore with some help and then proceed to organize their government. Through such a policy the American Government and the American Colonization Society coöperated for about twenty-seven

[1] ". . . the whole coast was thought to be left open for the selection of a proper place. . . ." Message of December 17, 1819, *Messages and Papers of the Presidents,* II, 640 (House Mis. Document No. 210, pt. 2, 53rd Congress, 2d session, 1896).

years in nursing the Liberian Republic into existence.[2] Altogether the American Navy carried over 5,000 captured slaves to Liberia; the remainder of about 15,000 consisted of freed Negroes from the United States.

These ex-slaves were settled in what came to be called Liberia by agents of the American Colonization Society, under the leadership of white men who served as governors of the colony, chief of whom was Jehudi Ashmun. The first colonists arrived off the west coast of Africa in a government-chartered schooner. And the first purchase of land from Native chiefs was made in 1821 by an agent of the Society assisted by Captain Stockton of the U.S.S. *Alligator*. Despite agreements with Native chiefs as to the purchase of land, conflicts soon arose. And in 1823 Captain Spence of the *Cyane* arrived in Liberia to protect the settlers, recently attacked by the Natives, and to assist in building forts as future protection.

In 1825 a constitution for the settlement of Monrovia (named after President Monroe) was drawn up and approved by the American Colonization Society. Meanwhile other colonization societies were formed in America which established settlements along the Liberia coast. Except for Maryland, these settlements joined together in a central government in 1839, called the Commonwealth of Liberia. (Maryland joined in 1857.) This government was actually administered by the American Colonization Society. In 1836 Thomas Buchanan, a cousin of President Buchanan, came to Liberia as governor. The last of the white governors, he died in 1841, and was succeeded by an octoroon from Virginia, Joseph Jenkins Roberts, an able man.

When this Liberian republic started to levy duties on British trade, it got into trouble, for nobody had recognized it as a sovereign state. In a note to the United States, August 9, 1843, the

[2] It is interesting to note that President Monroe, who was to lay down the non-colonization doctrine for Latin America in the Monroe Doctrine, should have pledged the United States, in the message of 1819, to non-colonization in Africa.

President James Buchanan, in his annual message of December 6, 1858, referred to the recent capture by a United States brig of an American slaver, with 306 Negroes, under the Act of 1819. He then said that ". . . no express provision was made for their protection and support after they had reached the place of their destination." He did not accept the narrow interpretation of this Act that such slaves might be "landed by our vessels anywhere in Africa and left exposed to the sufferings and the fate which would certainly await them." So he made an agreement with the American Colonization Society to settle these slaves in Liberia for the consideration of $45,000. *Ibid.*, V, 527–28.

British Government said it wanted to know "what degree of official patronage and protection, if any," did the United States extend to the "colony" of Liberia. In reply Secretary of State Upshur said that the American Government regards Liberia as occupying a "peculiar position and as possessing peculiar claims to the friendly consideration of all Christian powers; that this Government . . . would be very unwilling to see it despoiled of its territory rightfully acquired, or improperly restrained in the exercise of its necessary rights and powers as an independent settlement." [3] In substance this has been American policy to the present day.

Meanwhile the American Colonization Society found itself in an anomalous position. It was a private society attempting to run a government. It decided to withdraw so that Liberia could be recognized as a sovereign state. In 1847 the settlers in Liberia held a convention; drew up a constitution, modelled on that of the United States; and adopted the motto, "The Love of Liberty Brought Us Here." Britain quickly recognized the independence of this Negro republic, followed by other powers but not the United States. No doubt because of the slavery issue we recognized Liberia only in 1862.[4]

With the withdrawal of the American Colonization Society, Liberia was left to shift for itself. White men had already withdrawn as governors of the "colony" and the responsible relationship to Liberia of the American Government, under the Act of 1819, came to an end. Our warships periodically went to the rescue of the Monrovia authorities when confronted by tribal uprisings, as in 1852 in the case of the *John Adams,* and again in 1875. Moreover, American missionary organizations, together with the colonization societies, continued to send in thousands of dollars a year which helped keep the country afloat. But after guiding the destinies of this new state for its first twenty-seven years, responsible direction from the outside abruptly ceased. A Liberian writer says, "We question very seriously the appropriateness and the expediency of such an experiment." [5]

[3] *Affairs in Liberia,* U. S. Senate Document No. 457 (61st Cong., 2d sess.), p. 60.

[4] At that time we made a treaty with Liberia, Article VIII of which authorized our intervention against the aboriginal inhabitants, at the request of the Liberian Government. This treaty was "supplanted" by the Treaty of Friendship, Commerce and Navigation concluded between the two countries, August 8, 1938. Article XXIV. *Treaty Series No. 956.* (*See* Appendix 1.)

[5] E. J. Yancy, *op. cit.,* p. 56.

Liberia was founded in an epoch when liberals believed that a people, no matter how poorly prepared for freedom, could achieve it more quickly if thrown upon its own resources than if obliged to go through a period of tutelage by more advanced peoples. The history of Liberia does not support this contention. The descendants of the original Americo-Liberians may have a sense of freedom lacking in Negroes under colonial rule. But the Liberians have made much less economic, cultural, and political progress than the American Negro. Nor is this surprising. In the light of our present knowledge of the cultural and material differences between primitive and advanced groups, and of the dangers in uprooting an individual from his cultural environment, it is almost miraculous that 5,000 captured African slaves and about 15,000 freed Negroes from America should have succeeded as well as they did in making a new life for themselves in West Africa. Having diverse African backgrounds and languages these people were suddenly dumped into an entirely strange spot, marked by a severe tropical climate, great economic difficulties, and struggles with Native tribes and foreign powers. It is an astonishing achievement that these people should have been able to maintain, particularly after the withdrawal of American direction in 1847, an independent Negro state. No doubt the policy thereafter followed by the United States had something to do with this—weak as this policy may have been; but luck and ability on the part of the Liberian leaders, with all their defects, must be given their due.

Throughout the rest of the nineteenth century Liberia experienced difficulties with its Native tribes, some of whom raided British and French colonies; with Britain and France, who demanded that such raids stop and who succeeded in obtaining part of Liberia's original territory; and with foreign creditors. In 1871 Liberia secured its first foreign loan (with a London banking firm), receiving only a small part of the $500,000 actually borrowed, a sum soon squandered. Believing that President E. J. Roye had personally profited from this transaction and fearing his attempt to extend his term of office illegally, the Liberian Legislature deposed him and soon stopped interest payments.

In 1879 France offered to place Liberia under its protection; but the State Department in Washington declared it felt a "peculiar interest in any apparent movement to divert the independent political life of Liberia, for the aggrandizement of a great continental power." But when the British Government proposed that both Britain and the United States "make a joint declaration of special interest" in the independence of Liberia, the United States shied away from any guarantees. In difficulty again over its boundaries, Liberia in 1908 itself proposed a joint guarantee which the United States again declared was "impracticable."

Meanwhile in 1906 Liberia once more found its finances in chaotic shape, and obtained another $500,000 loan. Through the medium of Sir Harry Johnston, the African explorer, Liberia negotiated this loan in London, part of which was turned over to the Liberia Development Company, Johnston's rubber plantation in Liberia, for the construction of roads and other purposes. Liberia also employed British officials in the customs administration and Frontier Force. A series of difficulties nevertheless arose between the Company and the Government which led the British to demand that Liberia enact sweeping reforms. Fearing British absorption, Liberia turned to the United States for help. The British were not enthusiastic about American assistance. They expressed doubt whether "there is at the present time any scope for the coöperation of the United States Government in the customs or police," although there might be room for an American judicial adviser.

Nevertheless in 1909 the American Congress authorized a commission to go and investigate Liberia's affairs. This body in its report proposed that the United States make a treaty with Liberia establishing there an American customs receivership similar to that in Santo Domingo. It also proposed an American loan with which Liberia could refund its British debt; an American naval coaling station, and American aid in training the Liberian Frontier Force.

The State Department doubted whether the United States Senate would approve a treaty providing for such a receivership, and it feared that Britain and other powers would not withdraw from Liberia in favor of an exclusive American plan. Consequently it took the initiative in working out a plan of using private finance, from a number of countries, to establish outside control. In 1912 American and European banking groups agreed to loan $1,700,000 to Liberia at 5 per cent, to mature in 1952. Nearly all of the 1912 loan went to pay off bad debts. The service of this loan was a first charge on the customs, the collection of which was placed in the hands of a foreign receivership. The General Receiver, who was also made Financial Adviser to the Liberian Government, was "designated" by the

President of the United States and "appointed" by the Liberian Government. Three other receivers were designated respectively by Britain, France and Germany. Although the receivership was technically international, the receivers were not responsible to any international agency but only to their respective governments. And disagreement between the receivers, as well as between the receivers and the Liberian Government, soon arose.

With the outbreak of World War I, Liberia's foreign trade was disrupted; customs fell off about 50 per cent; and the Government could not pay its 1912 obligations or meet local salaries. These burdens were superimposed upon a government hardly able to meet its ordinary responsibilities.

Meanwhile, in 1915 the Kru people went on a rampage, killing several Liberian customs officers. Had the Kru won this war, it was believed they would have placed themselves under British protection. Fear of British intervention increased when H.M.S. *Highflyer* arrived in Monrovia in the midst of the Kru revolt and offered its services to the Liberian Government. At the request of the Monrovia authorities the United States asked the British to withdraw. The United States now sent the U.S.S. *Chester* with arms and ammunition to Monrovia. Thus supplied, the Liberian Frontier Force decimated the Kru, while the Government hung numerous chiefs. Although the *Chester* itself did not fire upon the rebels, it did patrol the coast, transport Liberian soldiers, and forestall foreign intervention.

The United States had made its support of the Government dependent upon the adoption of far-reaching reforms. But having hung the Kru chiefs, the Monrovia Government was slow to clean house. His patience tried, Secretary of State Lansing sent a note to the American Minister in Liberia, April 4, 1917, which stated:

> The Department [of State] has in the past made known to the Government of Liberia through your office its disappointment in the administration of Liberian affairs, and the time has now arrived when this Government, as next friend of Liberia, must insist upon a radical change of policy. The Government of the United States can no longer be subjected to criticism from other foreign Powers as regards the operation of the loan agreement, and can no longer tolerate failure on the part of the Liberian Government to institute and carry out necessary administrative reforms.
>
> Unless the Liberian Government proceed without delay to act upon the advice and suggestions herewith expressed, this Government will

be forced, regretfully, to withdraw the friendly support that historic and other considerations have hitherto prompted it to extend.[6]

The note contained suggestions of reform, such as giving the General Receiver increased powers with respect to traffic in arms and ammunition; proposing changes in interior administration; financial reforms, and numerous other improvements. It also proposed that the granting of concessions should be greatly restricted, although no concrete proposal was made giving a veto to the Financial Adviser over such concessions. The note closed with the injunction, "while the Government of the United States will cheerfully accept promises in connection with the above enumerated reforms, it will not be satisfied with promises alone, tangible and permanent results must follow."

Subsequently the Liberian Government adopted these reforms for the most part, but they proved to be "promises"—not "results." Nevertheless we continued to assist in keeping order. Thus the United States Army officers at the head of the Liberian Frontier Force completely overcame a two-year revolt of Native tribes in the region of Cape Palmas, in 1919.[7]

The Bank of British West Africa, the only bank in the country at that time, had come to the aid of the Liberian treasury by advancing it a monthly sum to pay the local bills. In 1918 the Bank declared it could extend further relief only on condition that officials appointed by the Bank undertake a far-reaching reconstruction program, with the aid of a $15,000,000 loan with which the 1912 arrangement would be terminated.[8]

Liberia realized that the acceptance of such demands would make the Bank the dominant commercial and political power in the country. And back of the Bank stood the British Government. The Monrovia authorities thereupon again appealed to the United States. And the State Department induced the Treasury in September 1918 to open a credit of $5,000,000 to the Liberian Government, under authority of the First Liberty Loan Act of April 24, 1917, on the understanding that Liberia would accept a far-reaching reconstruction program directed by the United States (possibly modeled after that established by the United States in Haiti in 1915). On January 22, 1919 the Liberian Legislature authorized the President to accept the loan and to negotiate as to the plan. During the loan negotiations Acting Secretary of State Polk wrote, "It is against the policy of

[6] *Foreign Relations of the U. S. 1917,* I, 877.
[7] *Foreign Relations of the U. S. 1919,* II, 528.
[8] *Foreign Relations of the U. S. 1918,* II, 510ff.

this Government at the present time to permit the State of Liberia to be forced into a position where she will be dominated or controlled by any European Government or its agent." (*Ibid.*, p. 534.)

The next step was to approach Britain and France. The State Department did this in memoranda of November 19, 1918 in which it informed its allies that the United States wanted to convert the international receivership in Liberia into an all-American affair and to bring about reforms involving improved transport facilities, harbor improvements, better sanitation and the like. It declared that the 1912 plan had proved "expensive and cumbersome." As it stated later, "the multiple control of Liberian financial affairs" had not worked.[9]

Both France and Britain proved reluctant to give up the idea of international assistance to Liberia. Britain proposed that the rehabilitation of Liberia be brought before the Peace Conference. It also proposed, semi-officially, that the United States take an international mandate over Liberia. For its part the State Department tried to assuage the fears of Britain and France that the United States wished to establish a protectorate over Liberia, stating that its reform plan was "merely in the interest of good government" and to maintain "its historical position as Liberia's next friend." [10]

Britain proved less reluctant to withdraw from Liberia than did France. It agreed to do so provided equality of treatment was established and certain British claims satisfied. France, however, wanted to take over the German cable rights in Liberia; and made its withdrawal dependent upon United States support for a French concession to build a railway from Monrovia north into French territory at Beyla in French Guinea and also a port at Monrovia. The French proposed that the Liberian Government subsidize this construction in return for a share in the management. So far as is known this concession did not materialize, and the French finally approved the idea of American control. Both France and Britain, however, firmly told the United States that order must be maintained along their borders with Liberia. "The anarchical conditions in the hinterland are a source of constant expense and annoyance." [11]

[9] *Ibid.*, II, 545. Also *Foreign Relations of the U. S. 1919, The Paris Peace Conference* (1919), I, 548 (hereafter cited, *Paris Peace Conference*).

[10] *Paris Peace Conference*, I, 545, 548; *Foreign Relations of the U. S. 1919*, II, 476.

[11] *Foreign Relations of the U. S. 1919*, II, 476.

The United States advanced $18,000 to enable the Liberians to send a delegation to the Paris Peace Conference. Liberia was represented there by a mixed commission of Liberians and Americans, headed by a Liberian chairman, Secretary of State King.[12]

The United States was successful in keeping Liberia off the Peace Conference agenda, but it did take advantage of the presence of the Liberia delegation to negotiate a memorandum of agreement, signed June 15, 1920. Liberia agreed to place the collection of all Liberian revenue, the administration of Native and military affairs, and the control of virtually all government expenditures, in the hands of thirteen American officials in return for a United States Government loan of $5,000,000.

Had the United States promptly followed up this agreement, Liberia doubtless would have accepted its terms. But for some reason no action was taken, and Liberian opposition to American control arose. American officials believe that this opposition was inspired in part by "misrepresentation and intrigue" of foreign powers.[13] In May 1920, Washington sent the U.S.S. *Chattanooga* to Monrovia, a visit which, according to the American Minister there, proved "quite beneficial to American prestige." Later, following Liberian amendments to the plan, Secretary of State Colby telegraphed on August 2, 1920 that if Liberia turned down the plan it might be necessary for the United States "to reconsider its objections to the establishment of a mandate over Liberia."

Meanwhile, American Chargé Bundy in Monrovia was becoming impatient. Reporting that the Legislature was opposed to the agreement, he urged that another cruiser be sent; and on August 21, 1920 he said that United States assistance to Liberia made it "morally responsible for the perpetuation of a Government notoriously inefficient, corrupt, and hostile to effective reforms. . . . All American officials here except two are so unfavorably impressed by the gross carelessness, deliberate obstruction and quibbling of the Liberian Government that they have expressed to Legation desire to leave Liberia." Bundy had reluctantly reached the conclusion that nothing substantial could be done unless a mandate were established or effective intervention undertaken.

[12] This commission was instructed by President Howard to demand readjustments in the French and British boundaries and to secure the dissolution of the 1912 receivership in favor of the American plan. The President also confirmed the offer, first made in 1908, of an American naval coaling base in Liberia. *Paris Peace Conference,* p. 547.

[13] *Foreign Relations of the U. S. 1920,* III, 52ff.

Despite diplomatic pressure, supported by visiting American warships, Liberia remained stubborn. Secretary of State Barclay (note of August 21, 1920 to Chargé Bundy) objected to any plan which would give an American receiver a veto "upon the exercise of certain sovereign and constitutional powers by this Government and its constitutional officers." The Liberian Legislature meanwhile found that the scheme "violated the Constitution of Liberia." During 1919–20 the Liberian Government granted three concessions without consulting the American Financial Adviser, which produced an American protest.

While this wrangling was going on the state of war between Germany and the United States was declared at an end on July 2, 1921. The authority of the American Government to make war loans was thereby terminated, and Congressional approval for a Liberian government loan of $5,000,000 became necessary.

In October a new agreement was drawn up and accepted by the Liberian Government, increasing the number of American officials from thirteen to twenty-two. The charges for their salaries would have totaled $109,700 which, along with the $250,000 interest on the United States loan, would have been greater than the customs revenue of the country. Despite new cries that Liberia would lose its independence, the Liberian Legislature reluctantly accepted this plan in 1922, and the House of Representatives in Washington did likewise. The Senate, however, refused to do so, Senator Borah declaring the loan would simply pay off at par Liberian bonds purchased by private interests at 10 or 20 per cent.

Secretary of State Hughes on December 26, 1922 informed the Liberian Government that the failure of the loan "is not indicative of any change in the traditionally friendly attitude of this Government toward the Liberian Republic. This Government will always look with sympathetic interest at any attempts of the Liberian Government and people to promote the real interests of the Republic." [14] Once more the United States, even if employing suave language, had left Liberia in the lurch.

Liberia now returned to "normalcy" along with the United States. But American automobile concerns and the American Government were soon shaken out of their "normalcy" by the British Stevenson plan to boost the price of rubber. Determined to find a source of rubber supply not under monopolistic control, Mr. Harvey Firestone between 1924 and 1926 studied the possi-

[14] *Foreign Relations of the U. S. 1922,* II, 633.

bility of raising rubber in Liberia and elsewhere. From the Monrovia Government he asked for and finally obtained a 99-year lease for a maximum of 1,000,000 acres of land for the production of "rubber and other agricultural products." At the time a Firestone publication declared that this rubber concession, the largest in the world, would result in the investment of $100,000,000, the employment of 350,000 workers, and the production of 200,000 tons of rubber annually, or about half the world production at that time.[15]

Mr. Firestone, however, insisted that this rubber concession be made dependent on an American loan which would build up Liberia as planned under the 1921 agreement and get rid of non-American influence, represented by the three foreign receivers.[16] Apparently Mr. Firestone hoped that the American Government would revive the 1921 plan. But the State Department pointed out that Congress had not supported the idea. Mr. Firestone then proposed to make a private loan as an alternative. A memorandum of July 8, 1924 by an Assistant Secretary of State said:

> To any inquiry why they did not consider it possible to secure the necessary safeguards through appropriate provisions in their proposed rubber concession, the reply was made that they had in mind the failure of this Government to accord what they considered adequate protection to American investments in Mexico. It was also observed that there was not even the protection of the Monroe Doctrine in Liberia.

Liberia, however, did not look with favor on a proposed loan coming from Mr. Firestone. On April 28, 1925 Secretary of State Barclay wrote the American Minister:

> The fundamental position which the Liberian Government takes upon this question is that it is politically inadvisable in their view to place the Republic under financial obligations to any private concern operating in the country under grants from the Government. This is a line of policy from which there can be no departure. Secondly, in the changed conditions which now obtain in the country, no loan could be negotiated with a private concern upon the terms and conditions of the Agreement negotiated by the Liberian Mission to the United States in 1921. The reason being that any rights the Liberian Government, for political purposes, would be willing with every confidence to accord to the Government of the United States, or any obligations which they would be willing to assume *vis-a-vis* said Government, they can find

[15] R. L. Buell, *op. cit.*, II, 823.
[16] *Foreign Relations of the U. S. 1925*, II, 367, 379, 385, 404.

themselves able neither to accord nor undertake towards a private concern however well recommended.[17]

Barclay suggested that money be secured from sources other than a corporation operating in Liberia.

Mr. Firestone solved this problem by setting up a subsidiary called the Finance Corporation of America, which drafted a loan agreement. The American Consul General in Monrovia told the Liberian Government that the State Department "having carefully gone over the Firestone contract felt that all that had been previously contemplated in loan of 1921 might be accomplished through these Firestone Agreements."

Secretary of State Kellogg on May 1, 1925 urged the acceptance of the Firestone contracts by Liberia, saying the Department:

earnestly believes that the successful establishment of the rubber industry in Liberia will tend to promote the country's welfare. . . . Mr. Firestone has assured the Department that as soon as the contracts are in effect there will be money available for necessary public works such as roads and ports. Furthermore, the Department would be willing to give appropriate assistance and at the request of Liberia and of the American interests concerned would be prepared again to assist in the selection of a Receiver General of Customs.

The interest of the Department in the conclusion of these contracts may be taken by the Liberian Government as proof of its continuing friendly interest in Liberia. It would seem, therefore, most unfortunate should a disagreement as to the exact terms of a loan prevent or delay the conclusion of a contract which will in all probability be of immense advantage to Liberia.

Secretary Kellogg repeated such advice several times.

Nevertheless throughout 1926 the Liberian Government and the Firestone interests engaged in a rather acrid controversy over the terms of the proposed contracts. The Liberian Legislature, being anxious to preserve the "sovereignty" of the country and to avoid what it called the "Haiti Affair," in February approved the Loan Agreement, subject to some twenty-four amendments. This action tried Mr. Firestone's patience. On February 18, 1926 he wired the State Department, "They must accept agreements without [a] single change if we go into Liberia." He had already threatened to transfer his interests to Dutch Borneo and the Philippines.

Meanwhile, Liberia was involved in a boundary dispute with the French Government over the so-called Zinta sector. On July

[17] *Ibid.*, II, 381, 385, 425.

2, 1925 the American Minister in Liberia wrote: "It is believed that an indication from the United States to France that the American Government would look with disfavor upon any further aggression by the French Republic . . . would once for all put an end to a long standing difficulty and settle a question of territorial sovereignty." At Monrovia's request the State Department (October 13, 1925) offered its good offices in connection with this dispute.

The Liberian Government feared, however, that if it turned down the Firestone contracts the American Government would withdraw its support of the Liberian Government in its controversy with the French. Although Acting Secretary of State Castle [18] was to deny publicly any connection between the two issues, Secretary of State Barclay privately wrote on April 28, 1925 to the American Minister as follows: "Frankly, what it has been hoped the Republic would gain from the encouragement of large American investments in the country is a counterpois[e] to other menacingly aggressive interests already established in this country, a balancing of foreign influences here and a new economic impulse." [19]

Whether for this or for other reasons, the Liberian Government finally came to terms. In addition to the Plantation Agreement already mentioned, the Liberian Government made the Loan Agreement of 1926 with the Finance Corporation of America, a Firestone subsidiary. The latter undertook to make a forty-year loan to the government of Liberia of a maximum of $5,000,000 in order to refund the 1912 loan held by European and American bankers and to secure economic development. This is one of the few refunding loans in history which actually increased the burden on the debtor government, for the interest rate was raised from 5 to 7 per cent and the life of the loan extended from 1952 to 1966. Only the first half of this loan in fact was issued. It went largely to the paying off of the 1912 loan and the internal floating debt. In addition, about $36,000 went to repay the United States for the expenses of the Liberian delegation to the Paris Peace Conference and certain other items advanced by the United States Treasury. In repaying this advance Liberia gained the distinction of being with Cuba the only government in the world to pay in full the war debt to the United States—an achievement, according to Secretary Mellon,

[18] *New York Times,* August 31, 1928.
[19] *Foreign Relations of the U. S. 1925,* II, 424.

"that bears a glowing tribute to the ability of her statesmen and to the industry of her people as a whole." [20]

In accepting the Loan Agreement Liberia got rid of the three European receivers, but it was obliged to accept in return eight officials headed by a Financial Adviser designated by the President of the United States. In addition to the Financial Adviser, five of these officials were to concern themselves with financial affairs, while two Army officers from the United States were to administer the Liberia Frontier Force. For twenty years, moreover, Liberia could make no refunding loan without the consent of the Financial Adviser. Thereafter the Finance Corporation had an option on any new loan.

A third agreement provided that Firestone would build a harbor at Monrovia at a cost not to exceed $300,000 which the Liberian Government would repay. Mr. Firestone engaged J. G. White Engineers who expended more than $115,000 on the project, but concluded the "shifting sands made the project impracticable except at prohibitive expense." [21] The work was abandoned, the cost being absorbed by Mr. Firestone. Eighteen years later the port project was revived, its construction being undertaken under the direction of the United States Navy. Today the United States Government plans to spend $12,500,000 on this port.

The grant of land made by the Liberian Government to Mr. Firestone was more generous than he could have secured in any other part of the world, and the terms of the 1926 loan were severe. Service charges and advisers' salaries amounted to a fixed charge of nearly $270,000 a year, constituting 20 per cent of government revenues in 1928, and about 50 per cent in 1931.

The 1926 loan proved as unproductive as the loans of 1871, 1906, and 1912. More than 90 per cent of the $2,500,000 advanced by the Finance Corporation went to pay off existing obligations, the remainder being left for sanitation and public works. Moreover, according to some writers, the land grant appeared to be a violation of the Liberian constitution which prohibits any alien from "holding" real estate, a phrase which the Liberian Supreme Court has in several cases interpreted to prohibit any concession for more than twenty years.[22]

The Liberian Government accepted these terms partly because it wished the infusion which the Firestone investments would

[20] *Foreign Relations of the U. S. 1927,* III, 168. (*See* Appendixes 5 and 6.)
[21] James C. Young, *Liberia Rediscovered* (1934), p. 36.
[22] N. Azikiwe, *Liberia in World Politics* (1934), pp. 158–61.

bring to the country, and also because it felt the need of the firm diplomatic support of the American Government against the designs of more powerful neighbors.

To a certain extent its hopes in both respects have been realized. Not only has Liberia stopped having trouble with France over its boundary, but the Firestone rubber enterprise has proved the only real productive venture in the country. Imports jumped from $2,252,000 in 1926 to nearly $4,850,000 in 1928, for the most part representing Firestone investment.

Nevertheless, new difficulties arose between Liberia and the United States. In 1929 an epidemic of yellow fever broke out causing the death of the American Minister, William T. Francis, Dr. James L. Sibley, Educational Adviser to Liberia, and other foreigners. Representations were made to Liberia by the American and other governments, as a result of which Dr. Howard F. Smith of the U. S. Public Health Service was loaned to Liberia. After staying eleven months he was withdrawn by the American Government. In a note of December 12, 1930 the United States representative frankly stated, "Because of the lack of coöperation on the part of the Liberian Government and officials this work has been unproductive." [23]

In 1930 the Finance Corporation of America declined to make further advances on the loan, except for $18,000, charging nine specific violations by Liberia of the Loan Agreement. League experts investigating conditions in 1931 found that large sums, supposedly devoted to the construction of the Monrovia-Kakata road, had been diverted to the construction of private houses. Although the Loan Agreement prohibited the creation of a floating debt (Article XV) the government proceeded to accumulate such a debt, which reached $680,000 by December 31, 1932. It was in the following year that the American Government made its blistering indictment of corruption and inefficiency in the Liberian Government (see page 36). Dissatisfied with the financial policy of the Government, the Bank of British West Africa withdrew from Monrovia, being eventually replaced by the Bank of Monrovia, Inc., a Firestone subsidiary.

Meanwhile reports multiplied that conditions of slavery and forced labor existed in Liberia on a large scale. President King and also the State Department at first denied these charges.[24]

[23] Department of State, *Liberia: Documents Relating to the Plan of Assistance Proposed by the League of Nations* (1933), p. 32.

[24] The charges with respect to general conditions in Liberia and the dangers of forced labor if Firestone actually developed his million-acre concession

As the charges were reiterated, Mr. Stimson, who had recently become Secretary of State, telegraphed the American Minister in Monrovia on June 5, 1929 that the reported situation in Liberia as to forced labor "justifies earnest representations."

> It would be tragically ironic if Liberia whose existence was dedicated to the principle of human liberty should succumb to practices so closely akin to those which its founders sought forever to escape.
>
> The Government of the United States, because of its century-old friendship for Liberia, is impelled urgently to call the attention of the Liberian Government to this matter and to impress upon it the vital importance and necessity of reforming without delay the social conditions reported to exist, and the Government of the United States does not doubt that the Liberian Government will be prompt to appreciate the situation and to take all appropriate measures to this end.[25]

Subsequently the State Department proposed that Liberia appoint an international commission of inquiry to investigate these charges. Although the United States in 1921 and 1926 had worked to oust other nations in Liberia in favor of exclusive American control, the State Department now agreed to coöperate in an international inquiry and later (in 1931) in an international reconstruction program. Subject to the pressure of the American Government and public opinion generally, Monrovia in April 1930 announced the creation of a commission of inquiry consisting of one member named by the United States, a second by the League of Nations, and a third by the Liberian Government. After a visit to Liberia this commission summarized the results of its investigation in a report completed in September 1930 and published in January 1931. It reported numerous abuses, the gravest of which was an organized system of forced labor in connection with the nearby Fernando Po cocoa plantations. It charged that officials and relatives of President King received a fee of $45 for every "boy" thus recruited, and that Liberian officials, including Vice President Yancy, actually

were first made at Williamstown by R. L. Buell, *New York Times,* August 30, 1928. Following two cables from Acting Secretary of State Castle (published in 1936 in *Foreign Relations of the United States 1928,* III, 249, 250) urging him to do so President King of Liberia denied these charges in a telegram to the State Department. Acting Secretary of State Castle also made a public reply (*New York Times,* August 31, September 1, 1928). However, the International Commission of Inquiry sent to Liberia (C.658, M.272, 1930, VI) declared that among other sources of information used by the Commission were books: "In recent years the most notable reference is that which appears in Raymond Buell's 'The Native Problem in Africa.' "

[25] *Foreign Relations of the U. S. 1929,* III, 274, 275.

sent Liberian soldiers to "catch" boys for this purpose. The Commission also reported excessive forced labor with respect to the road program, and grave abuses in the administration of the Native tribes.

After reading this report Secretary Stimson informed President King that the United States was "profoundly shocked." He demanded prompt reform. On November 17, 1930, the State Department sent a second note declaring that nothing had been done to carry out reforms and no action had been taken to punish the guilty officials. The note continued, "unless there is instituted by the Liberian Government a comprehensive system of reforms, loyally and sincerely put into effect, it will result in the final alienation of the friendly feelings which the American Government and people have entertained for Liberia since its establishment nearly a century ago." [26]

Confronted by this threat, President King and a number of other officials abruptly resigned in December 1930, ostensibly because of opposition to their "reform" program. Secretary of State Edwin Barclay became Acting President, being subsequently elected to the presidency on May 28, 1931. The United States said that its decision with respect to recognizing the Barclay government would depend to a considerable extent upon the attitude taken by Liberia toward the report of the international commission.[27]

Although President Barclay declared that he would not surrender Liberia's independence in accepting outside assistance to clean up conditions, the Liberian Legislature did enact laws prohibiting the export of labor and pawning, creating a public health service, and reorganizing the administration of the hinterland. Such measures were largely international window-dressing. For at the beginning of 1932 the American, British, and French Governments informed the League of Nations that the Monrovia Government had "massacred" hundreds of Kru people by way of reprisal for testimony before the International Commission. Investigation showed that while this was not true, a revolt of the Kru had broken out. This revolt was induced by unscrupulous Liberians who told the Kru that as a result of the international inquiry the white man was going to take over the country and they did not need to pay taxes. There is no evidence that the Monrovia Government punished such Libe-

[26] Texts published in League of Nations, *Official Journal,* February 1931, pp. 467–68.

[27] G. H. Hackworth, *Digest of International Law,* I, 306.

rians, but Liberian troops as in 1915 proved guilty of grave excesses in repressing the rebellion.

In December 1930 the Barclay government presented to the League of Nations at Geneva the report of the slavery commission. Confronted by these serious charges as well as by an increasingly difficult financial situation, due in part to the depression, the Liberian Government was virtually obliged to ask assistance from the League to give effect to the recommendations of the Commission. The League Council thereupon set up a Liberia Committee, consisting of representatives of eight member states. The United States accepted an invitation to join the Committee.

There were two problems before this Committee. The first was to work out a program of League assistance for Liberia. The second was to secure a modification of the 1926 Loan Agreement so as to ease the financial situation of the Liberian Government.

In September 1932 the League Committee adopted a plan of assistance based largely on a report of three experts sent to Liberia in the previous year (the so-called Brunot Report). Following two protests from the United States that the original project did not go far enough in delegating authority to foreign officials, the League plan was strengthened.

During the negotiations the Liberian representatives fought hard against any proposal to fasten real control on their country. They declared they could not accept any assistance plan which involved the political organization of the country, or placed the administration of its Native population in the hands of foreigners. Liberia did, however, finally agree to the League plan of assistance in September 1932 on condition that negotiations with the Firestone interests lead to a satisfactory outcome.

The League plan of assistance provided that the League Council should "designate" three provincial commissioners, three deputy commissioners, and two medical officers, who then would be "appointed" by the Liberian Government. The whole territory of Liberia would be divided into three provinces and administered by the provincial and deputy commissioners. The total salaries of these officials, including the Chief Adviser mentioned below, and the other expenses of the program would be $150,000 a year. To guarantee these charges a working capital of $150,000 should be created for the unexpended balance of the 1926 loan. In addition to these League officials, the American loan officials, including the Financial Adviser, would continue in existence.

To coördinate the work of the foreign officials in Liberia, the League plan called for the "appointment" (not "designation") by the League Council of a Chief Adviser with the agreement of the Liberian Government. This Adviser could not be of the same nationality as that of the Financial Adviser or of the powers holding neighboring colonies. This ruled out an American, Britisher, or Frenchman. On October 9, 1933 the United States accepted this proviso, if with some reluctance.

Under the League plan the Chief Adviser was authorized to prepare, in collaboration with the President of Liberia, a detailed plan of assistance. The Liberian Government should agree to act in accordance with his advice and recommendations; but if it wished to refer any disagreement to the League Council it could do so. The decision of the Council would be final, provided it acted by unanimous vote except for the vote of Liberia. The Monrovia Government should also agree to "grant to the Chief Adviser ample and sufficient authority for the effective execution of the plan of assistance." In particular, he could ask for any documents and official reports and make investigations. The Chief Adviser should also arbitrate disputes between the American Financial Adviser and the Liberian Government. The Chief Adviser should report quarterly to the League Council. Should the latter body find that the Liberian Government had disregarded its promises, the Council could declare that the protocol had lapsed, and that the modifications to be made in the 1926 Loan Agreement for the benefit of Liberia would also automatically come to an end.

Meanwhile the Finance Corporation was not satisfied with the League plan and sent a vice-president to Monrovia to make a report. Shortly before his arrival, on December 23, 1932, the Liberian Legislature enacted a moratorium on the Firestone loan until government revenues reached $650,000 annually for two consecutive years. This idea had been taken from the plan drawn up by the League experts, but the League moratorium had been contingent on the inauguration of a real international reconstruction program, which had not yet been agreed on. At the same time the Liberian Government dismissed the Acting Financial Adviser, and committed a series of other acts which violated the 1926 Loan Agreement. Despite the protests of Firestone, the League Committee, and the State Department, Liberia failed to rescind these measures. The growing concern of the United States was indicated when in March 1933 the President sent Major General Blanton Winship as his representative on special mission to Liberia.

Despite the Liberia moratorium, the Finance Corporation proceeded to negotiate a revision of the 1926 agreement. It accepted a reduction in the interest rate from 7 to 5 per cent, and agreed that the current expenses of government and the cost of the assistance plan would have priority over the cost of servicing the Firestone loan which had priority under the 1926 agreement. The Corporation also agreed to renounce interest when Liberia's annual revenue amounted to less than $500,000 a year, and undertook for five years to guarantee the salaries of the foreign advisers when they could not be met out of current revenue—and also agreed to make a $150,000 loan as initial working capital. Firestone agreed to make these modifications in the 1926 loan contract on two principal conditions: first, that Liberia repeal its moratorium and other unilateral legislation which violated the 1926 Loan Agreement and, second, that Liberia accept the League plan of assistance as strengthened.[28]

In June 1933 the Liberia committee accepted eight out of the twelve changes in the plan of assistance required by the Firestone interests as "sufficient guarantees." These strengthened the authority of the Chief Adviser over the provincial commissioners; and provided that a two-thirds majority rather than a unanimous vote of the League Council was to govern decisions of the League Council with respect to the application of the plan. Finally, the Committee accepted the Firestone insistence that the Chief Adviser be an American.[29]

In addition to recommending changes in the Loan Agreement of 1926, the League committee of experts had criticized the vast extent of the Firestone rubber concessions. In its second preliminary report to the League Council, the Liberia committee stated that in the opinion of certain of its members "the coexistence in Liberia of a weak State and a powerful foreign undertaking gives rise to disadvantages."[30] The Liberia committee subsequently recommended that the size of the Firestone

[28] Two other conditions were stipulated by Firestone: (1) that Liberia recognize the Depository Agreement between the Liberian Government and the U. S. Trading Company Banking Department; and (2) that Liberia agree to amortize the floating debt without recourse to internal bonds.

[29] This provision, however, was eventually rejected by the Committee. See p. 38.

[30] League of Nations, *Official Journal,* March 1932, p. 524.

concession be reduced by negotiation, assisted by League experts, and the land rental increased from 6¢ to 50¢ an acre.[31]

Nevertheless, in its final report the League Committee made no recommendations concerning the Plantation contract. Instead, a League expert, Mr. Ligthart, officially reported that:

> I understand from the Firestone Plantations Company's representative that it is prepared to make the utmost possible allowance for the general interests of Liberia, and that it would be perfectly ready, in consideration of the well-being of the population, to take account of competent opinions. In particular, I understand that the Firestone Plantations Company, during the operation of the plan, will be glad to consult with the Chief Adviser and the Provincial Commissioners concerned in the selection of additional land.

And the Liberia committee finally said that the question of permanent modifications in both the Loan and Plantation contracts was a matter for negotiation between the parties concerned.

League officials at the time had doubts about their reconstruction program. Its first weakness was lack of financial support. It saddled the Liberian Government with the salaries of outside officials but did not provide the country with the funds needed for its real development. Moreover, the League plan would not have supplanted the American control over Liberian finance under the 1926 agreement, despite the provision that the Chief Adviser should arbitrate disputes between the Financial Adviser and the Liberian Government. It was doubtful whether the dual system of control would have worked.

Nevertheless, on November 19, 1933 the State Department issued a statement saying:

> The American Government expects Liberia to accept the Plan of Assistance and will be pleased in this case to coöperate in its successful execution. Should the present administration at Monrovia reject this opportunity, such action could only be construed as opposition to reforms the urgent desirability of which has been apparent for over three years, and as indifference to the welfare of the million and a half native people of Liberia.[32]

Meanwhile the Liberians followed the tactics they had pursued in 1920 and 1921. Although they accepted the first plan

[31] League of Nations, *General Principles of the Plan of Assistance,* C/Liberia/17(1), May 1932.

[32] Department of State, *Liberia: Documents Relating to the Plan of Assistance Proposed by the League of Nations* (1933), p. 1.

of assistance, they now charged that the revised plan was a violation of Liberia's constitution and sovereignty. Liberia rejected the new financial proposals outright. The League of Nations by this time had lost its patience. The League Council formally withdrew its offer of a plan of assistance in May 1934. Thus, the three-year effort of the League of Nations and the United States to put Liberia on its feet came to nought. Liberia had succeeded in playing off the League, the United States and Firestone against each other, and the Liberian governing class had won.

Britain, however, continued to take the matter seriously. The British delegate to the League Council suggested that, in view of the Liberian Government's treatment of the Natives, which violated Article 23 (b) of the League Covenant, the Council would be entitled to consider Liberia's expulsion from the League; and the British Ambassador in Washington was instructed on May 29, 1934 to say to the American Government that even the threat of exclusion from the League would not be adequate to bring about real improvements in Liberia.

> They are aware of the deep interest which the United States Government have always taken in the fortunes of this State, which, indeed, owes its foundation to American enterprise and philanthropy. On the material side, Liberia is rendered dependent upon the United States Government by the extent to which her financial machinery is already in American hands and organised in conformity with a contract entered into between the Liberian Government and an American corporation. His Majesty's Government cannot, therefore, doubt that the United States Government have been as much perturbed as have they themselves by the course of recent events, and they would be grateful for an indication of the policy which the United States Government would in the circumstances recommend. For their own part, His Majesty's Government are ready to co-operate to the utmost of their power in any well-considered measures which the United States Government may consider appropriate to the occasion.[33]

So far as the public knew, the State Department made no reply to this communication. In July 1934 it did send to Monrovia for a special investigation, Mr. Harry A. McBride of the State Department who had been Financial Adviser and General Receiver of Customs in 1918. (Mr. McBride subsequently negotiated the Defense Areas Agreement of 1942. See Appendix 2.)

Despite his rejection of the League plan, President Barclay realized that he could survive only if recognized by the United States. Consequently, at the time of the withdrawal of the

[33] *Papers Concerning Affairs in Liberia,* Cmd. 4614 (1934), p. 52.

League proposal, the Liberian representative at Geneva made a declaration saying, "So definite . . . is the Liberian Government's determination to secure the advice of Specialists in its administration that it has decided to obtain them otherwise than under the plan of assistance." In his annual message of October 26, 1934 the President added that in pursuance of this declaration, "which the Government regards as an international engagement," two specialists had already been employed.

In August the President drew up a three-year plan for international development, approved by the Legislature in December. At the same time the Legislature authorized the President to negotiate a modification of the 1926 Loan Agreement.

Under the three-year plan the President engaged eight "emergency" specialists, mostly American; but these specialists lacked power and got into interminable difficulties with the Liberian Government officials. They did serve as international window-dressing. When the three-year plan expired in December 1937, their contracts were not renewed. The only foreign advisers who at present remain in Liberia are the American loan officials now reduced to three, who today have very little authority, and the military advisers.

Shortly after the adoption of the three-year plan, President Barclay came to terms with the Firestone interests. On January 1, 1935 the so-called Supplementary Agreement No. 1 (supplementary to the 1926 Loan Agreement) was concluded between the Liberian Government on the one hand and the Finance Corporation of America and the National City Bank of New York on the other. The preamble of this agreement referred to the three-year plan and to the pledge of Liberia to retain the services of competent foreign specialists, the majority being Americans. Applying ideas worked out by the League reconstruction plan, the agreement provided that Liberia need not pay current interest on the Firestone loan when annual revenue fell below $450,000, the so-called Basic Budget. This budget covered the salaries of the loan officials and advisers, in addition to ordinary administrative expenses. Interest on the 1926 bonds was reduced from 7 to 5 per cent, but only to December 31, 1942. Moreover, should government revenues rise above $450,000 the excess should be applied to pay current interest, but if not sufficient, the balance would be cancelled. Revenue above what was needed to pay the interest should apply to amortization and also to the liquidation of the floating debt which on December 31, 1934 stood at $650,000. Finally, the Liberian Government promised to issue bonds to the amount of $355,000 to clear up interest payments due as of January 1, 1935. At the end of three years (December 31, 1937) the provisions of the 1926 agreement would be automatically revised. The Supplementary Loan Agreement No. 1 would enter into effect only if the Liberian Legislature repealed the moratorium of 1932 and other acts which violated the 1926 agreement. This the Liberian Legislature proceeded to do.

Several months later (March 20, 1935) Liberia and the Firestone Plantations Company concluded Supplementary Plantations Agreement No. 1 (supplementary to the Plantations Agreement of 1926). This enlarged the tax exemptions granted Firestone. Liberians state that the value of these new tax exemptions is much greater than that of reducing the interest rate from 7 to 5 per cent. But this overlooks the fact that in return for such exemptions the Firestone interests returned to Liberia cancelled bonds of the value of $650,000. Of this amount, $400,000 represented an advance on land rent, while $250,000 was in connection with tax exemption. In addition the Firestone Plantations Company received the right to operate a radio communications system and an aerial transport system on its land, and also the "exclusive right" to take up by mining the "mineral contents of the subsoil" under its leased land, subject to a royalty not exceeding 10 per cent on "precious metals or stones."

Apparently satisfied that Liberia had met its obligation and enacted internal reforms, the United States recognized President Barclay in June 1935. The British followed in December 1936. Liberia thus surmounted the gravest crisis in its history, escaping from foreign political control.

No doubt heaving a sigh of relief, President Barclay declared in his Inaugural Address of January 6, 1936:

> Liberia, and Liberians in the past few years, have had to pass through the crucible of both responsible and irresponsible criticism. This has thrown into high relief their real and fancied deficiencies. The severest self-analysis will not leave us unconvinced that some of that criticism was just. This experience will have been without benefit if it has not developed in us the courage to face realities. We should not, therefore, hesitate to shed that self-complacency with which we have been so strongly inhibited in the past, and secure that assistance and adopt competently recommended methods as will assure the strengthening of our National Institutions, the broadening of our social activities and the proper basing of our Nation's economic life.

With the approaching expiration of Supplementary Loan Agreement No. 1, the parties concluded a second agreement November 10, 1937. Supplementary Loan Agreement No. II continued the interest reduction five more years, but was less generous than the first agreement in providing that when revenue fell below $475,000, the interest due should be paid in bonds, instead of being cancelled. Supplementary Loan Agreement No. III was concluded December 28, 1939, continuing existing provisions, and providing for a schedule of payments in the event that Liberian revenues should go above $525,000 (as they did during World War II). Moreover, it authorized the Firestone Company to pay its land rental and revenue tax direct to the National City Bank until such time as the Liberian loan had been discharged.

Meanwhile the Firestone Plantations Company secured new rights in Supplementary Plantations Agreement No. II of December 1939. Thus, the Company received the right to construct communication and transportation lines, including a "railway" outside the land leased under the 1926 agreement. The lessee merely promised to "consult" the government in the matter of the "location" of such lines. The Company was also granted the right to use government land not already devoted to some other "incompatible" use for rights-of-way, not to exceed 80 feet in width, and for station-areas not to exceed five acres.

At the end of 1944 the parties "permanently amended" the Loan Agreement of 1926, replacing the supplementary contracts. This reduced the interest rate from 7 to 4 per cent until the beginning of 1950, and then fixed it at 5 per cent for the remainder of the loan. Although the loan continued as a first lien on customs, head money, land rent and rubber revenues, the contract provided that if the government receipts should be less than $565,000 a year, interest on the loan should be paid in bonds rather than cash.

The loan contract provides that the Liberian budget be divided into two parts: (1) the Basic Budget, amounting to $565,-000, for operating expenses, plus current interest and amortization on the Finance Corporation loan amounting to $145,000 a year, or a total basic budget of $710,000; (2) the second part of the government intake, which is called Excess Revenues. When government revenue equals a million dollars or more, the government may appropriate 90 per cent for the use of the Basic Budget, i.e., for its ordinary operations. The remaining 10 per cent is earmarked as follows: 10 per cent but not more than $35,000 for arrears in amortization; 23 1/3 per cent but not more than $35,000 to the government's floating debt; 33 1/3 per cent but not more than $50,000 to public roads; 33 1/3 per cent but not more than $50,000 to a Reserve Fund. In the event that the floating debt is paid, one-third of the excess revenue shall be applied to the "extension of the educational and sanitation facilities of the Republic." Thus when Liberian revenue is as high as it now is ($1,800,000 in 1944), the government has a substantial sum left for internal improvements.

In his annual message of 1938 President Barclay quoted the American Financial Adviser as follows:

> The Republic of Liberia, notwithstanding its great and urgent need of funds for the advancement of progress and public improvements in the Republic; the need of construction of roads and bridges over which to transport its national products to market, requirements for administrative purposes, and additional safeguards of the public health and sanitation, has constantly maintained its credit both at home and abroad. For the payment of its foreign and domestic obligations the Republic of Liberia contributes approximately twenty-five per cent of its income, and has consistently operated under a budget of appropriation not in excess of that proportion of the National Income allocated to its own purposes. . . . Both foreign and domestic debts have been reduced in amounts which considering the income of the Government, have been large. The position of the Government of Liberia today in regard to its national credit is worthy of the highest admiration.

Mostly responsible for Liberia's good credit are the Firestone interests and the National City Bank, tacitly supported by the State Department.

Nevertheless, it is a striking fact that at a time when Liberia was virtually required to keep up its interest payments, if at a reduced rate, and to balance its budget, the State Department made no protest when Latin American governments went into partial or complete default to American bondholders. On the contrary, the American Government through the Export-Import Bank actually extended to these countries new credits. In the case of Liberia, however, the State Department recognized President Barclay only after he had agreed to resume interest payments. The American concerns involved could not be blamed for taking advantage of this situation. What was lacking was a United States policy.

In any case, in a period of history when the American Government was itself engaged in a colossal deficit financing, Liberia enjoys the distinction of having maintained a balanced budget since 1935. Except for Cuba, it is the only government in the world to pay in full its war debt to the United States. Moreover, today all the arrears on the 1926 loan are paid off; the internal debt will be wiped out in two years; and it is hoped that the foreign debt as a whole will be extinguished before 1966, the date originally fixed.

Chapter IV

RECENT ECONOMIC DEVELOPMENT

Apparently to offset Firestone influence, and to quicken the development of the country, President Barclay tried to induce European interests to enter the country. Thus, in 1931 the Government granted in a preliminary agreement a concession to the Danish-Liberian Syndicate to build a pier in Monrovia, and a 99-year exclusive right to build a motor-truck road from Monrovia to the Franco-Liberian boundary. The government agreed to set aside 75 per cent of the harbor dues to pay for the construction of a customs house; and authorized the Syndicate to collect a charge on the traffic passing over the road of which a small percentage was to be returned to the Government. The Government leased up to 40,000 acres of land at 50¢ an acre to the Syndicate, agreeing that no traders could trade within a mile of the trading stations erected by the Syndicate without its consent. In return for these rights and certain tax exemptions, the Syndicate agreed that the Liberian Government could "participate financially in the different undertakings for an amount of twenty-five per centum of the value, which is to be fixed by a mutual understanding between the Syndicate and the Government." In the British House of Commons the question was raised whether this concession was not a monopoly which would make British commerce in certain areas of Liberia illegal. Whether or not because of pressure from British or American sources, this concession was not put into effect.[1]

A new effort to enlist non-American capital was made in August 1937 when the Liberian Government approved a mining agreement with the *Noord Europeesche Erts En Pyriet Maatschappy,* giving it a concession to prospect and develop the Bomi Hill iron fields, and obliging it to construct at its own expense a harbor basin either at Monrovia or Cape Mount. Ships belonging to the company would be exempt from harbor and other dues during the life of the agreement; NEEP would pay a tonnage royalty of 4¢ a ton on iron ore, if the price f.o.b. Monrovia

[1] Azikiwe, *op. cit.,* p. 342.

did not exceed $3.00, rising proportionately thereafter.[2] Later it was discovered that Axis capital was back of the Dutch concern; and no doubt because of American pressure the concession was cancelled the following year without arousing any protest from the Netherlands Government. Thus, a further effort of Liberia to secure the construction of a port came to an end.

By 1933 Liberia showed signs of recovery. In 1934 imports increased to $1,233,158 from the low point of $858,741 in 1931. In the same period, however, exports fell from $679,885 to $555,656. This fall was due largely to declining prices, palm kernels dropping from £15 a ton to £5 in 1933; coffee from £38 to £14. Resenting these prices, Liberian producers in Grand Bassa boycotted the merchants until some price increases were made.

World War II did not disturb Liberia nearly as much as World War I. The disruption of European shipping and the British navicert system did cause a decline in relatively non-essential exports, coffee and palm oil each falling off nearly 100 per cent. Nevertheless, trade as a whole boomed, rubber constituting 92 per cent of the exports, gold coming second with 4 per cent. Imports increased from $2.2 million in 1938 to $3.3 million in 1941. Exports shot up even more, rising from $1.9 million to $5.0 million in 1941. By 1944 exports rose to $10,139,000 while imports touched $3.8 million. During the last several years Liberia has converted a passive into an active balance of trade.

As the result of World War II, Liberia has increased its dependence upon the United States with respect to its foreign trade. In 1942, the United States took $7,922,000 out of $9,-282,000 of Liberia's exports, and provided nearly all its imports. Moreover, in 1941 government revenue was nearly twice that of 1934. In 1941 it hit the million-dollar mark and increased in 1942, despite the disruption of non-essential exports. Liberia so far has escaped the grave financial difficulties encountered in World War I and again in 1932.

This economic prosperity has been largely due to the wartime activities of the Firestone Plantations Company, and to a lesser extent to those of the Pan American Airways and to the expenditures of the American military forces in Liberia.

[2] *Acts . . . of the Republic of Liberia,* 1937, pp. 42ff. This prints only the Legislature's amendments to the mining concession, but not the full text. For its repeal, see *ibid.,* 1938, p. 9.

The Firestone Plantations Company represents the one concrete evidence of economic progress in Liberia since 1926. Its operations to date have proved more modest than at first contemplated. Instead of actually leasing a million acres of land, the company has taken up less than 200,000 acres, of which 80,000 are under cultivation. Instead of employing 350,000 native workers, as a Firestone publication first predicted, it employs about 30,000, the actual force at work every day being about 26,000. Instead of producing 200,000 tons of rubber a year, it produced last year about 17,000 tons. Instead of investing $100 million in Liberia, it has invested about $15 million. Even so, this is the largest rubber operation in the world.

It takes about five years for a rubber tree to come into bearing; and it is understood that the Firestone Company is now tapping over 50,000 out of its 80,000 acres under cultivation. In fact the company has followed a policy of drastic tapping, i.e., of prematurely tapping the trees for the sake of the war emergency, even though the plantation is thereby injured. Liberian rubber has been of first-class importance to the American war effort. Except for Ceylon, Liberia was the principal source of plantation rubber under United Nations control. It is understood that regardless of the rise of synthetic rubber, the Firestone operations will be maintained in Liberia after the war—in fact these operations have been extended at the rate of about a thousand acres a year. All the Liberian rubber exported is consumed by the Firestone plant at Akron, Liberia providing only about one-quarter of its needs.

The Firestone Company has done something to encourage independent rubber production in Liberia. Thus, it provides free rubber seeds to independent growers and, what is more important, high-yielding clones, or buds, as well as trained men to open up plantations. About a hundred Americo-Liberians, among them ex-president King and Mr. James F. Cooper, and a few Natives, have started plantations totalling about 2,500 acres. In 1943 the independent producers exported about 100 tons.

The Firestone Company has the reputation of treating its workers well. The current African wage of 18 cents a day is paid, but in addition incentive bonuses are given for increased output. A company store sells food to the Natives at the 1941 price level. This in fact amounts to a subsidy because rice is sold at 3¢ a pound although its present imported price is 10¢. The amount of credit extended to Natives at the company store is strictly limited so the worker cannot get hopelessly into debt.

Work on the rubber plantations is pretty continuous throughout the year, but the workday is over by early afternoon. If the workers wish they can till their own gardens, land being provided for the purpose. Native workers are housed in villages made up of houses provided by the company, the Natives preferring a Native-type house made of frame construction with an earth plaster wall and a thatch roof. At each village is a dispensary, attended by a dresser trained at the hospital. The division superintendent, a white man, maintains a rigid inspection of water supply and other sanitation facilities. Firestone already has experienced labor shortages, and suffers from labor turnover. It has not succeeded in inducing many Natives to bring their families to live permanently in the company villages, as has *Union Minière du Haut Katanga* in the Belgian Congo, partly because of the attachment of the Natives to their chiefs, to their women and to tribal lands.

The Firestone Plantations Company has built two hospitals at a cost of $100,000, staffed by five American physicians. Its annual medical budget is about $200,000 a year. It has put into effect a compensation system for injured employees. It also operates a pre-natal clinic and a program of child care. The company maintains a school for the training of nurses from which fifty Liberian nurses have graduated, eight with post-graduate diplomas.

At present Firestone is operating a hydro-electric generating plant which can produce 1,500 K.W.H. of power, with Liberian employees trained by its engineering staff. It has carried on a broad research program in establishing a variety of food and other crops in its experimental gardens, pioneering in the growth of wet rice and high-grade tobacco.

The Firestone Company contributed $20,000 to the Harvard School of Tropical Medicine which in 1926 sent a research expedition to Liberia, publishing two volumes in 1930 called *The African Republic of Liberia and the Belgian Congo.* The company made contributions also for an anthropological survey, for a study of the tropical timber of Liberia and for the publication of a grammar of a leading Liberian native language, Kpelle. It contributes to the budget of the Booker Washington Institute. The Company has established a public radio service; has expended $275,000 on 125 miles of road within the plantation; and contributed $65,000 to the improvement of government roads. It has also organized and supported a sleeping-sickness mission.

Nevertheless, numerous criticisms of the Firestone operations are made by Liberians and others. Thus, it is alleged that about 125 Americans monopolize all managerial and scientific positions, and that no Americo-Liberians or American Negroes are employed in such a capacity. A former Firestone employee declares that Natives have been dispossessed of their land and traditional rice fields disrupted when rubber land was staked out.[3]

Liberians declare, moreover, that the Firestone Company is the only source through which the Natives can market and process their own rubber. They assert that Firestone abuses its monopoly position to pay Native producers less than the market price. They also charge that the plan of the Barclay government to collect wild rubber in wartime from the Natives independently of Firestone failed because of the Firestone fear that such trade would weaken its rubber monopoly.

They also contend that the Firestone contribution to Liberia's revenue is unduly small. By virtue of its tax exemptions, the Plantations Company pays no corporate income tax and no Firestone employee is subject to an income levy. The Firestone taxes are limited to 1 per cent of value (N. Y.) of rubber exported, and to 6¢ rent per acre a year on the land actually taken up. In 1938 President Barclay declared in his annual message that the Firestone taxes constituted less than 3 per cent of the government revenues. The company disputes these figures, pointing out that it pays several hundred thousand dollars' duty on imported goods sold at the company stores, and that its total tax contribution constitutes about a third of the government revenues.[4]

From this distance it is difficult to determine whether there is any basis for these criticisms. Given the general backwardness of the country, and the weakness and the inferiority complex of the governing class, any successful foreign corporation would be subject to criticisms, no matter how enlightened its social policy may be.

[3] Arthur I. Hayman and Harold Preece, *op. cit.*, pp. 78–79.

[4] In 1943–44 the company paid to the Liberian treasury a total of $435,037, of which the chief item was about $275,000 customs duties paid by the Firestone Trading Company on goods sold at the company stores; being followed by $94,179 paid out as a tax on rubber exports. The land rentals amounted only to $12,128 because such rentals had been paid up in advance on 110,000 acres for 99 years, because the Liberian Government badly needed current revenue. The company also pays the hut tax due by all Native workers on the plantation, which last year amounted to $12,170.

Inquiry, moreover, shows that the charges that Firestone is abusing its rubber "monopoly" are unfounded. The price of rubber in wartime has been fixed not by Firestone but by the U. S. Rubber Development Corporation in agreement with Britain. The price paid is 23½¢ a pound (it is believed that 15¢ rubber yields a profit), and the Development Corporation pays the Native producers exactly the same price as it does Firestone. It is true that the Rubber Development Corporation originally made an agreement with the Liberian Government with respect to collecting wild rubber. But President Barclay insisted that agents of the Corporation refrain from dealing with the Natives direct but, rather, employ the services of a government agency called the Liberia Export-Import Corporation, similar to the old Government Employment Bureau. Although President Barclay said the plan should yield 5,000 tons of wild rubber a year, in fact it yielded only 8 tons! The reason was the Liberian Government agents paid the Natives in worthless script, while pocketing the hard cash paid by the Development Corporation for the rubber collected. With the failure of the first wild-rubber program, the Rubber Development Corporation induced the Liberian Government and Firestone to make a new agreement, April 20, 1944, providing that Firestone should be the agent for the wild-rubber program with the right to employ thirty Liberian assistants at rubber stations established for the purpose. Assured of honest payment, the Native has an incentive now to collect wild rubber, and it is believed the new program will yield about 200 tons a year.[5]

The real criticism which can be directed against the Firestone enterprise is its vast potential size, namely, of a million acres of land, and the political influence it exercises through the 1926 Loan Agreement. Should the Firestone Company proceed to develop a million acres of land (instead of 80,000), and should it open mines and build railroads as it is entitled to do, what is now a potential monopoly would be converted into a real one with injurious results to the country. In the first place, an acute labor shortage would certainly develop to the disadvantage of the Native producers and other foreign concerns. Competition for labor might then arise which could lead to some form of compulsory labor and to the disorganization of Native life. Sec-

[5] The procurement officers of FEA experienced similar difficulties with a palm-oil program in Liberia. Partly because of the character of the Americans who organized the Liberia-America Corporation, the palm-oil program proved a failure.

ondly, the full use of the Firestone rights would work against the growth of a class of Native producers, which is essential to the economic and political independence of the country. The future of Liberia should not depend upon foreign corporations employing Native wage earners; there should be a place for a number of such corporations which, by example and technical assistance, stimulate Native production. But primarily the future of Liberia depends upon the growth of an independent Native middle-class.

Finally, the development of such a huge concession, virtually taking up the best land, would make it difficult for other foreign companies to enter Liberia. Now the United States Government has taken a strong position on behalf of the Open Door, particularly in China and the Middle East. On August 9, 1943 Mr. Henry S. Villard (now Chief of Division of African Affairs of the State Department) declared at Chautauqua that the United States has "no desire to carve out for its exclusive benefit any portion of Africa. . . . Our traditional policy of the 'Open Door,' if applied uniformly to all colonial areas, is one which we confidently expect will aid in removing sources of economic conflict."[6] In view of such a policy, it should be to the interest of the United States to see that the Open Door is applied with scrupulous care to Liberia, our "next friend." It is difficult to argue that Firestone's potential hold on Liberia conforms to the Open Door policy.

Given the absence of a responsible United States governmental policy, Mr. Firestone possibly was right in risking a large-scale investment in Liberia only on very generous terms. Assuming that the United States will now adopt a more responsible policy toward that country, the Firestone Company no doubt would be willing to revise its concession, as indeed it informed the League of Nations committee. If the United States Government decides to assume real responsibility toward this country, the Firestone Company should be requested to revise its rubber concession, limiting its holdings, say, to 200,000 acres instead of a million acres, and possibly increasing the land rental from 6¢ to 50¢ an acre, as the League experts proposed.[7] Likewise the 1926 Loan

[6] *Vital Speeches of the Day,* September 15, 1943, p. 723.

[7] In 1906 the government of British Malaya gave to Sir Frank Swettenham land for rubber cultivation in perpetuity at thirty cents of a Strait dollar quit rent annually per acre—somewhat less than the present rate paid by Firestone in Liberia. The Firestone Company believes its present rental of 6¢ is adequate since the price of land in the interior on the rivers is valued

Agreement should be replaced by an inter-governmental arrangement discussed later.

Upon returning home in September 1944, Mr. Lester A. Walton, American Minister to Liberia, declared, "Liberia is on the threshold of the greatest economic development in its history." [8] The American Financial Adviser in his report of 1942 does not share this optimism. On the contrary, he expresses apprehension about Liberia's postwar economic future. He pointed out that before the outbreak of war, Liberia was beginning to lose its export markets (apart from gold) because of poor quality of its products and poor marketing methods. Liberia had flourished because of the war boom, but at the end of the war there was danger that the Liberian economy would fall flat. He intimated that the country should increase the local production of food. Despite the law prohibiting imports of rice except in case of emergency, and the adoption of a protective tariff in 1935, the country still imported rice and other products which could easily be produced at home. In this category he mentioned fruits, vegetables, cotton, cooking fats, soap, sugar, lumber, furniture, and clothing.

The postwar economic welfare of Liberia depends upon whether new resources of wealth are developed, and how they are developed. The most obvious possibility lies in the exploitation of Liberia's iron deposits, which have interested several foreign groups in the past, without result. In December 1943 a United States Geological mission arrived in Liberia to survey these iron resources at the request of the Liberian Government. It reported that iron could be found in the Kpandemai Mountains, 180 miles north of Monrovia, near the French border, but that these deposits were too low grade and too small to be of any present commercial interest. But in the Bomi Hill area, about 40 miles north of Monrovia, it found high grade iron with a small amount of deleterious elements. The mission estimated that there were probably between 5 and 8 million tons of hematite-magnetite rock, possibly containing 60 per cent

only at 50¢ an acre by Liberian law. (*Revised Statutes of the Republic of Liberia,* Vol. II, Sec. 1285, Par. 4.) The question is, however, whether the land is not under-valued. The Liberian Legislature can increase the valuation when it wishes. The Liberian Rubber Syndicate has rented rubber land at 6¢ an acre. But that was before World War I. Since then the world has made progress in its sense of the treatment to be accorded undeveloped countries.

[8] *New York Times,* September 24, 1944.

of metallic iron, within 200 feet of the surface. Most of such iron could be scraped off simply by steam shovel.

To exploit such iron it would be necessary to build either a first-class highway or a railroad between Bomi Hill and the new port at Monrovia. The Liberian Government hopes to find American concerns willing to undertake such a construction as part of a concession to mine Bomi Hill and operate the new Monrovia port.

The opening of an iron mine will involve new and serious social problems. Such a mine can be exploited only by foreign capital and foreign entrepreneurs. Even if a foreign concern adopts an enlightened social policy and agrees to pay a substantial royalty to the Liberian Government, the development of iron mining will increase the drain on the Liberian labor supply, along with foreign influence in the country. Unless such a development is accompanied by real economic and social rehabilitation, with a view to increasing Liberia's population and the number of independent small farms, the political independence or social welfare of Liberia will not necessarily be advanced by new foreign operations.

These mining and railroad developments are still in the realm of theory. Meanwhile a foundation for postwar progress has been laid, which did not exist before World War I, namely, the Firestone operations and the construction of a modern port by the United States. The question is whether the new policy of the United States, indicated not only by this port but also by the dispatch of the economic and public health missions to Liberia, is adequate to meet Liberia's future needs.

From the standpoint of foreign capital there are a number of obstacles to activity in Liberia. The first is a tropical climate. The wet season in Liberia begins about the first of April and runs until the last of November. There are two or three weeks in July, however, known as the "middle drys." The dry season as such falls in the winter months. "Liberia has one of the rainiest and most humid climates in Africa." [9]

The rains in Liberia are severe, at times descending like machine-gun fire on the galvanized iron roofs of the houses of Monrovia. Total annual rainfall may go over 170 inches a year.

[9] Dr. Richard P. Strong (ed.), *The African Republic of Liberia and the Belgian Congo* (1930), I, 27. (The observations of the Harvard African Expedition, organized by the Department of Tropical Medicine.) Another authority says, "West Africa had a very sinister reputation in the matter of health." Lord Hailey, *op. cit.*, p. 1117.

As the result of moisture, the climate of Liberia is enervating. During the rainy season the temperature remains fairly constant, about 80 degrees; but during the dry season it is more varied. In the middle of the day the temperature has been known to register 105 in the sun, dropping to 65 during the night, and a blanket is sometimes necessary. If one keeps out of the sun during the middle of the day, the weather is not as oppressive as New York or Washington during the summer. Moreover, during part of the dry months, the land breeze, called the *harmattan,* blows in from the Sahara Desert.

Diseases common to Africa are sleeping sickness (borne by the tsetse fly) and malaria (borne by the mosquito), together with leprosy. In the French and British colonies on the west coast, governments have developed important public health services. As a result, these colonies have been pretty well cleaned up. But Liberia has no public health service worthy of the name. In contrast to the public health service of Sierra Leone colony, just to the north, which has fifteen European medical officers and 160 African dispensers, there is one good doctor in Monrovia and no independent doctors elsewhere. The missionary organizations, the Firestone Company, the Pan American Airways, and of course the American Army units in Liberia, provide their own medical service.

From time to time the most deadly of tropical diseases has appeared in Liberia—yellow fever (also carried by the mosquito). This caused the untimely death in Liberia of Dr. James L. Sibley, a promising American educator. Lord Hailey's *An African Survey* declares (p. 1127), apparently on the authority of the Rockefeller Foundation, that Liberia is "a permanent reservoir, from which the diseases can be carried to adjoining territories." The Liberian Government vigorously denied this statement.

Foreigners are frequently harassed by petty and frivolous suits brought by Liberians against anyone with a little money. This condition is due largely to the fact that in the past the educated Liberian has known no occupation except that of "lawyer," due to the tradition against manual labor and the lack of economic opportunities. Hayman and Preece write:

> Possibly no modern country, with the exception of Nazi Germany, has ever established a judiciary with such arbitrary powers over helpless individuals [here the authors are referring to Natives] as this unknown nation. . . . Perjury, discrimination, unmitigated harshness emphasized by pomp and deceit—these are the cornerstones of a legal system which

makes the most corrupt court in the United States seem like a tribunal of wisdom and mercy by comparison.[10]

Mrs. Elizabeth D. Furbay, wife of the former head of the College of West Africa, also writes:

A native workman at the school [Booker Washington Institute] had just been "converted" in a revival in nearby Kakata. When he was caught stealing carpentry tools from the school and the principal had said, "I thought you were a Christian and that I could trust you," the thief immediately sued his employer for defaming his character. The suit was not the first or the last of its kind brought against him. In each case the guilty person was supported by minor Government officials.

To take another example:

A native, riding on the school truck, jumped from the moving vehicle into the path of another car and was killed. Although the driver of the school truck was eventually absolved from any blame, the school's American director received a letter from a high Government official saying that the matter could be settled with him for $150. An itemized account of the costs attached to settling the affair was requested by the principal, but his letter was never answered, indicating that the official was only trying to use his authority (not connected with this case) to extort money from an unwanted white man.

A garage belonging to the school was found missing. It had been torn down and completely removed in one night. Another high Government official, without communicating with the school, had ordered the building removed because he decided it was "too near the road." [11]

The same writer relates how an American missionary woman

had received word from a Liberian lawyer that her washman was suing her for slander and was asking two hundred dollars redress. A few days previously she had discharged the man for dishonesty and now he was retaliating with this charge. She had no witness to support her; neither did the servant; but that was of no importance for he would get one of his tribal brothers to swear that he had heard Mrs. Newell call him a thief—and the word of the "witness" would stand in any court.[12]

In the old days such difficulties would have been solved by inducing the Liberian Government to accept extraterritorial or American courts to try Americans in Liberia. Such courts had jurisdiction over American troops for the duration of the war, but as a peacetime proposition there is no possibility of

[10] *Op. cit.*, p. 54.
[11] *Top Hats and Tom-Toms,* pp. 251–52.
[12] *Ibid.*, p. 88.

their being established. Meanwhile, the court harassments will probably increase with the growth of Liberian nationalism directed against the foreigner. In the long run, economic development should give productive outlet to Liberians now engaged in shyster practice, but in the immediate future the situation can be improved only through the firm diplomatic intervention of the American Minister and by a different United States policy toward Liberia mentioned below.

Another obstacle to foreign activity is discriminatory labor legislation. Several years ago President Barclay quickly secured the enactment of a so-called Wage Act which increased wages from 50 per cent to 200 per cent for every employer in Liberia, except the government. Since Firestone was the only large foreign employer in Liberia, probably out-ranking the government itself, this law was obviously aimed at that company. If enforced, it would have made their operations very difficult. The measure in fact was discriminatory, and was obviously unjust. Nevertheless, the State Department did not protest against the Wage Act, as Firestone wished, because it at the time was accused of supporting an anti-labor policy in Bolivia. Liberia is not the only undeveloped country which expresses its mounting nationalism by labor legislation imposing very heavy charges on foreign operations. Outright discrimination against foreign employers no doubt is a violation of international law; but the State Department has not been very successful in protecting American oil interests in Bolivia and Mexico from expropriation. The best assurance that Liberia will not follow such examples, and re-enact similar wage acts, is a strong diplomatic policy on the part of the United States, as well as an enlightened social policy on the part of American capital operating in the country.

Another means of making foreign capital virtually untenable in a country such as Liberia is the imposition of oppressive and discriminatory taxation. To protect itself against such burdens, the Firestone Planting Agreement of 1926 (Article 2, Sec. A and B) provided that all "products" of the plantations and

> all machinery, tools, supplies and buildings established, constructed or placed upon the leased land or elsewhere for the operation and development of the Lessee's land holdings and all leasehold interests, improvements and other property, franchises, rights and income shall be free of and exempt from any internal revenue or other tax, charge, or impost except the revenue tax. . . . It is understood and agreed that this exemption shall not apply to Lessee's employees, labourers or servants.

It further provided that "all machinery, tools, and supplies of all kinds purchased and imported" for the operation of the Firestone development (interpreted to mean hospital supplies and games for the welfare of its employees) "shall be exempt from all customs duties or other import duties."

The agreement stipulated two taxes which Firestone would pay: (1) a revenue tax equal to 1 per cent of the value of the rubber exported, (2) a land rent of 6¢ per acre of land selected by the Company.

Moreover, the mining concession granted in 1937 to the *Noord Europeesche Erts en Pyriet Maatschappy* stipulated that a royalty of 4¢ a ton on iron ore f.o.b. Monrovia would be paid if the price per ton did not exceed $3.00, increasing by one cent per ton on every twelve-cent increase above $3.00.

The Treaty of Friendship, Commerce, and Navigation made between the United States and Liberia, August 8, 1938, provided that "The nationals of either High Contracting Party within the territories of the other shall not be subjected to the payment of any internal charges or taxes other or higher than those that are exacted of and paid by nationals of the State of residence." [13] It is not difficult, however, for a government to impose taxation technically non-discriminatory but actually bearing down chiefly on foreign enterprise.

In an effort to secure protection against possible abuse, the Firestone Planting Agreement of 1926 provided that differences between the Company and the Government should be referred to three arbitrators, one nominated by the President of Liberia, one by Firestone, and a third by the Supreme Court of Liberia. In case either party was dissatisfied as to the decision, it might apply for a further arbitration to be arranged by the Liberian Government and the United States State Department.[14]

The Loan Agreement, moreover, provided that disputes over the loan contract should be arbitrated, each party appointing an arbitrator. In case of disagreement, the Liberian Government and United States Secretary of State should collaborate as to planning a basis for final decision.

It does not appear that the arbitration provisions have ever been invoked by the Firestone Company. In any case, it would seem that in the postwar world American capital is likely to venture abroad only if the American Government is prepared to insist on certain minimum standards of justice.

[13] Department of State, Treaty Series, No. 956, Article I, second paragraph.

[14] Article IV (n) of the planting agreement, text in R. L. Buell, *op. cit.*, II, 886–87.

Chapter V

THE NEED FOR A FRESH APPROACH

America cannot escape perhaps the major share of responsibility for the difficulties which Liberia has experienced from the beginning. For the first twenty-seven years of the history of this republic, the American Government coöperated with philanthropic societies in getting Liberia started. Then America left it in the lurch—except for philanthropic handouts, mostly misspent, and periodic hands-off warnings to foreign powers, coupled with demands that Liberia reform itself.

Liberia tried to get on its feet with the aid of foreign loans in 1871, 1906, 1912, and 1926. All these loans proved unproductive for they went to pay off previous obligations to the benefit of Native and foreign speculators. Moreover in 1912 Liberia found itself saddled with a foreign receivership consisting of foreign officials coming from four different states. During World War I, the Wilson Administration attempted to take advantage of its war powers to get rid of the international receivership of 1912 and establish a virtual American protectorate over Liberia. But somebody delayed too long; the war powers expired and the United States Senate said No.

A few years later Liberia, determined once more to enlist American support—this time against French territorial demands—made the Firestone contracts of 1926. The State Department hoped that a private corporation could now do for the country what the American Government in 1921 had tried to do, and what the British and French Governments were doing in adjoining colonies. The American Government agreed to designate American officials authorized by the 1926 contracts, and in certain cases to arbitrate disputes between Firestone and the Liberian Government. Nevertheless, the American Government insisted that the Firestone contracts were "a private matter." [1] The American Government thus disclaimed any responsibility for the welfare of Liberia, placing the load on a private corporation which it could not be expected to bear. The American officials appointed under the 1926 agreement have had little

[1] See letter of April 18, 1934 of J. F. MacVeagh to Secretary of State Stimpson, *Annual Message of the President of Liberia,* 1934.

authority. Their chief success has been the collection of interest on the foreign debt.

In its relationship with Liberia the American Government is confronted with a so far unsolved dilemma. Liberia is an independent republic, yet it is in drastic need of outside aid which it hitherto has been unwilling to accept. The American Congress, and indeed the State Department, is committed to the principle of "non-intervention" in the affairs of other people. Having burned our fingers in the Haitian intervention of 1915, the United States has not confronted its responsibilities to Liberia but has tried to shove them on to a business corporation, just as before World War I the State Department made use of Wall Street banks to extend American influence both in the Orient and in Central America.[2]

As the result of World War II, a new Liberian policy seems to be emerging, namely, through the construction of the Monrovia port and the dispatch of several governmental missions. Indeed, history seems to be repeating itself. For just as the Wilson Administration attempted to make use of its war powers in 1918 to impose a postwar protectorate on Liberia, so today the United States Government is taking advantage of lend-lease to build and administer a port in Liberia, which in fact will be a naval base.

Several criticisms may be advanced against this new policy. First, it is doubtful whether the use of lend-lease for the construction of a postwar port is legal. Section 3(b) of the Lend-Lease Act, as amended on May 17, 1944, provides: "that nothing in this paragraph shall be construed to authorize the President to assume or incur any obligations on the part of the United States with respect to post-war economic policy, post-war military policy or any post-war policy involving international relations except in accordance with established constitutional procedure." [3] Certainly the construction of the Liberian port involves postwar "obligations" on the part of the United States—an obligation which in fact commits us to the future defense of Liberia. The Act of June 30, 1944 making lend-lease appropriations [4] did

[2] Dollar diplomacy was "an attempt to force American capital by diplomatic pressure into a region of the world where it would not go of its own accord." A. Whitney Griswold, *The Far Eastern Policy of the U. S.* (1938), p. 146. Mr. Firestone was more ready to go into Liberia than Wall Street was into China and Central America; but the net result remains the same.

[3] Public No. 304, 78th Congress, 2d session.

[4] Public No. 382, 78th Congress, 2d session.

not earmark any item for the Liberian port, and no mention of this Liberian development was made in the House hearings of March 1944 on the extension of the Lend-Lease Act, although it is understood that members of the House Appropriations Committee were privately informed of the port development. This is in contrast to the acquisition of the American naval base at Guantanamo which was authorized by Article VII of the Act of March 2, 1901, preceding the Executive Agreements of February 16, 1903 and July 2, 1903.[5] It is in contrast to the Act of June 30, 1944[6] in which Congress authorized the President to obtain postwar bases in the Philippines. Congress has passed no such act with respect to Liberia.[7]

No doubt the Administration will succeed in its new policy with respect to Liberia, in contrast to the failure of World War I, for the Liberian port will probably have been completed out of existing funds before Congress gets around to asking any questions. Nevertheless, to those who believe in the democratic control of foreign policy, the present situation represents part of the ominous trend toward Presidential dictatorship. The construction of the Liberian port should be approved either by a joint resolution of Congress or by treaty.[8]

Existing legislation probably authorizes the sending of the economic and public health missions to Liberia.[9] As far as the

[5] W. M. Malloy, *Treaties, Conventions, International Acts, Protocols and Agreements between the United States of America and Other Powers* (1910–1938), I, 358.

[6] Public No. 380, 78th Congress, 2d session.

[7] The assertion that the United States Government is taking advantage of lend-lease to build and administer a port in Liberia, which in fact will be a naval base, is open to other interpretation. Article 7 of the Agreement between the United States of America and Liberia for the Construction of a Port and Port Works, signed at Monrovia on December 31, 1943, does grant to the United States "the right to establish, use, maintain, improve, supplement, guard and control, in part or in their entirety, at the expense of the Government of the United States of America, such naval, air and military facilities and installations at the site of the port, and in the general vicinity thereof, as may be desired by the Government of the United States of America for the protection of the strategic interests of the United States of America in the South Atlantic." However, no lend-lease funds are being used specifically for the construction of naval facilities in the port. The port is designed for commercial purposes although under the terms of the agreement the United States Navy could use its facilities if it should ever decide to do so. [Ed.]

[8] In March 1944 the House discussed the Monrovia Port in closed committee hearings and, presumably, approved it. [Ed.]

[9] The Act of May 25, 1938 (Public No. 545, 75th Congress, 3d session) authorizes the President upon agreement with the government of Liberia

public knows, it is uncertain whether the Liberian Government has granted these missions power merely to make investigations, or also to execute an economic and public health program.

Our new Liberia policy is not only of dubious legality but it represents piecemeal administration. About a half dozen government agencies in Washington have Liberian sections, each trying to work out its own policy toward this republic. The people in charge of these sections are able and well-meaning. In theory these various agencies are coördinated by the African section of the State Department. But this coördination needs to become vigorous.

The final criticism to be directed against the new policy is that it does not go far enough. The only thing really tangible about it is that the United States will have a permanent strategic hold on Liberia after the war. Apart from the vague powers of the public health and economic missions, there is nothing as yet to indicate that the United States will make any thorough contribution to the solution of Liberia's grave economic and political problems.

With the right to maintain "military facilities" at Monrovia, the American Government will find it much more easy in the future than in the past to underwrite the existing Liberian oligarchy with all of its weaknesses.

As the result of this port development there is no likelihood that the United States now will wash its hands of Liberia and allow Britain or France to take it over. We are in Liberia to stay. Supposedly we will have a choice between the so-called "realistic" policy of merely protecting our strategic and rubber interests in the country, along with the governing oligarchy, and a policy of taking over the country either as an American protectorate or a mandate. But examination shows that neither course is desirable or possible. The problem is to find some alternative which, while protecting American interests, will really set Liberia on its feet without converting it into a colony.

The importance of finding an alternative that is not either mere protection of our strategic and rubber interests or outright political annexation is fortified by the considerable social and political progress made in colonial Africa between the two

(and the American republics and the Philippines) to detail to it for temporary service persons having special scientific and other technical knowledge. Moreover, Title III of the Appropriations Act of June 30, 1944 (Public No. 382, 78th Congress, 2d session) authorizes expenditures of lump sums for the travel expenses of employees of the Foreign Economic Administration.

wars. During this period many African colonies have enacted social legislation; created wage-fixing machinery; encouraged labor unions and Native coöperatives; established a system of labor inspectors; and showed a real concern over native education, nutrition, and public health.[10]

Moreover, the British Parliament has adopted a policy of frankly subsidizing colonial developments. The idea of a colonial subsidy is not new; between 1921 and 1943 the British tax-payer contributed nearly £38,000,000 to pay colonial deficits.[11] But the British Parliament created in 1940 a ten-year colonial development fund to be used not to pay off government deficits but to secure positive development of resources and the welfare of the Natives.[12] In British West Africa appropriations from this fund have been made to train Native teachers, specialists in agriculture, and to set up a veterinary training school. Such funds have also been used to construct a pilot sawmill; survey the juvenile delinquency problem; and to establish an Institute of West African Arts, Industries and Social Services.[13]

In addition to this social progress, political developments of importance have taken place in British West Africa within recent years. On the Gold Coast a new constitution has been promulgated which creates for the first time in Africa an elected majority in its Legislative Council. It is true that the Governor can override the decisions of the Council in the interest of "public order, public faith or good government"; but certainly the Gold Coast constitution is an important step toward African self-government.[14]

Moreover, a new constitution for Nigeria, where the principle of indirect rule, or of government through Native chieftains, has been developed more than in any other place in Africa, attempts to give the Native authorities direct participation in the central

[10] *Social Policy in Dependent Territories,* International Labour Office (1944); L. P. Mair, *Welfare in the British Colonies,* Royal Institute of International Affairs (1944).

[11] Sir Bernard H. Bourdillon, "Colonial Development and Welfare," *International Affairs,* July 1944.

[12] In 1945 a new Colonial Development and Welfare Act was passed. It allocated £120,000,000 for the ten years beginning April 1, 1946. £5,000,000 were set aside for research only. [Ed.]

[13] *Colonial Development and Welfare Act, 1940: Report on the Operation of the Act to 31st October, 1942.* Cmd. 6422, 1943. *Ibid.: Return of Schemes made under the Colonial Development and Welfare Act . . . to 31st March, 1943.* Cmd. 6457, 1943.

[14] *The Economist,* London, October 14, October 28, 1944.

Nigerian Government. Under the proposed new constitution, Nigeria will be divided into three provinces, each representing distinct sociological groups. Each region will have a House of Assembly, having an unofficial majority. Most of the latter will come from the Native authorities. These regional assemblies can make recommendations to the central Legislative Council, having twenty official and twenty-nine unofficial members. Sixteen of the latter will be nominated by the Native authorities in these Houses of Assembly. A House of Chiefs is also created in the case of the Northern Provinces only. Today in Nigeria not a single member of the Legislative Council represents traditional Native authorities; but under the new constitution, two-fifths of the Legislative Council, one-third of the Houses of Assembly, and every member of the House of Chiefs except the President will do so.[15] These proposals have been vigorously criticized by some Nigerians on the ground that the chiefs will be appointed by the British Government and therefore under its control. Nevertheless this is an interesting attempt to bridge the gap between the educated Nigerian intelligentsia and the traditional tribes—an experiment which Liberia would do well to study.

Finally, in October 1944 the British Government created a Standing Central African Council having a permanent secretariat, with consultative powers to promote coöperation as between the two Rhodesias and Nyasaland with respect to all matters of development and welfare, such as communications, health, and education. Direct African representation on this Council is envisaged.

Despite their struggle for self-preservation, the Free French found time during World War II to consider far-reaching revisions in their African policy. Thus, in January 1944 a colonial conference convened at Brazzaville, attended by eighteen Governors-General and Governors, which drew up resolutions looking to the creation of a French colonial federation; the increase of Native rights; and the recognition to a far greater extent than in the past of the importance of preserving and developing native institutions and traditions.[16]

Meanwhile, the Negro both in America and Africa is awakening. Particularly in British West Africa a Negro nationalist

[15] *African Transcripts,* July 1945; "Proposals for the Revision of the Constitution of Nigeria," Cmd. 6599, March 1945; Sir Bernard Bourdillon, G.C.M.G., "The Future of Native Authorities," *Africa,* July 1945.

[16] For the English text of the Brazzaville resolutions, see *Free France,* Special Issue No. 2, September 1944.

movement is beginning to emerge for the first time in history. Thus, the West African Students Union demands internal self-government for West Africa. A. A. Nwafor Orizu demands virtual independence for Nigeria.[17] In Nigeria a trade-union congress was formed in 1943, which has invited a group of American labor leaders to visit the colony.[18] No doubt it will be many years before self-government in British West Africa is realized because of the lack of a common language, and the presence of an illiterate population split up into numerous tribal compartments.[19] Indeed, if self-government came too soon in British West Africa, the result might be merely to create new Liberias. Nevertheless, the Negro nationalists of West Africa already are critical of the Americo-Liberian dictatorship and its exploitation of the Native tribes. A white defender of the Liberian tribes goes so far as to propose that Liberia surrender its independence to a West African federation which will insure to each tribe the right to develop its land and culture.[20] Certainly Africans themselves will advance such demands sooner or later, if Liberia does not soon become more democratic.

In World War II, African troops have fought in the Middle East, Madagascar, Italian East Africa, Ceylon and Burma. The war has given new opportunities and experiences to these Africans. About 12,000 Africans from Kenya alone have learned to operate motor vehicles. The East African Army Education Corps has produced about 500 Africans trained as teachers, information officers, welfare workers, interpreters, and Swahili instructors. An Army newspaper has been published in Swahili, called *Askari*, with a weekly circulation of 8,000. "Tens of thousands of soldiers have advanced farther during five years of war than would have been possible in two decades of peace." [21]

As a result of his war experience, the African is going to make demands which he did not make before the war. Sooner or later African nationalism is going to affect Liberia. Such nationalism, while believing in the independence of Liberia, will oppose the Americo-Liberian dictatorship.

Finally, the American Negro is showing a new interest in world affairs, particularly in the condition of Negroes outside

[17] Nwafor Orizu, *op. cit.*, p. 158.

[18] *New Africa*, October 1944.

[19] Julian Huxley, "What West Africa Needs," *New Statesman and Nation*, June 17, 1944.

[20] Hayman and Preece, *op. cit.*, p. 242ff.

[21] Russell Smallwood, "Native Military Development in East Africa," *The Fortnightly*, November 1944.

the United States. For example, the National Association for the Advancement of Colored People has hitherto restricted its activities to the American Negro. But in 1944 the Association appointed a committee on the Negro in the coming peace conferences. The American Negro is coming to realize that fascism abroad threatens to undermine Negro gains at home. But this does not mean that the American Negro will defend conditions in Liberia. On the contrary, he is becoming concerned lest the capacity of Negroes everywhere be judged by conditions in Liberia. Upon returning from a visit to that country, a Negro writer, Mr. George Schuyler, declared that the United States should undertake "benevolent supervision" of its affairs. Another American Negro, Dr. George W. Brown, wrote in 1941:

> "The Land of Liberty" definitely fails to justify the modest hopes of strong sympathetic western friends. . . . Accusations of extortions, bribes, petty grafting, court and legal corruption, flagrant abuses against the persons and property of individuals by soldiers or minor officials, misappropriation of funds, and "selling out the country" continue to revive among the unsavory charges made within and against the Republic.[22]

A Negro writer in the *Daily Worker,* November 16, 1944, stresses the need for internal democratic reforms.

Moreover, Mrs. Eslanda Goode Robeson, in her recent book *African Journey* (p. 28), writes:

> Liberia was to be the country where freed Negroes were to be really free, and were to help develop and educate their African brothers. And what happened? In time the freed Negroes (Americo-Liberians as they are called) followed the pattern of other colonial peoples—exploiting and enslaving the Africans, the Liberians. Considering the high purpose for which this black colony was founded, and the brave democratic principles upon which this now so-called republic is supposed to rest, the backwardness, poverty and lack of franchise among the subject Liberian people as against the wealth and official corruption among the ruling Americo-Liberian citizens makes a shameful picture—a disgrace to the "Republic" and to the United States which sponsors it.

Certainly the old romantic idea about Liberia is no longer held by the American Negro. When President Barclay and President-elect Tubman visited this country in June 1943, two leading American newspapers, the *Afro-American* and the *Chi-*

[22] George W. Brown, *The Economic History of Liberia* (1941), pp. 213, 214.

cago Defender, were quite critical of them as representatives of the Negro race.[23]

The Americo-Liberian oligarchy cannot count on support from the American Negro. It is only a matter of time when the latter will demand that Liberia reform itself, or, if this is not possible, that Liberia accept real American assistance. A few American Negroes now frankly believe that the United States should "take over Liberia."

Surrounded by new political and economic developments in neighboring colonies, and by a rising tide of Negro nationalism, Liberia continues to remain a stagnant pool, except for a temporary war boom. It can show no record of social progress, despite its "freedom." And its freedom is not real, for the aboriginal majority is not "free." It does not follow that the United States should annex Liberia. No doubt the colonial powers would welcome such a development; for the extermination of Liberia's independence would constitute a setback for all Negro independence movements elsewhere on the continent. Moreover, the racial chauvinists would hail such a development as proof of Negro incapacity everywhere, including the United States.

The United States, however, cannot continue to close its eyes to conditions within Liberia. American opinion is vocal in demanding "colonial reforms" in every part of the world. It demands freedom for India and the extension of the trusteeship system in Africa. Inevitably, if this keeps up, the British, French and other governments who bear colonial responsibilities will turn and ask the American people: "How can you continually criticize our policies when in Liberia, which is your especial responsibility, the majority of the people is probably worse off than in any other part of Africa?" The United States cannot answer such a question merely by repeating the phrase "non-intervention" and "self-determination." In the present world, Liberia's independence can be maintained only if it meets the responsibilities of independence.

[23] The *Afro-American* of June 19, 1943 criticized the appearance of President-elect Tubman, and carried a sub-title, "Salary $30,000; Native Wages 25 Cents a Day." The *Chicago Defender* of June 5, 1943 said that President Barclay's 28-word speech to the United States Senate would long be remembered for its "painful stupidity." See also E. E. Johnson, "The Liberian State Visit," *The Crisis,* October 1943.

Chapter VI

A LIBERIAN REHABILITATION PROGRAM

The problem of reconciling Liberian independence with an effective program of American assistance is difficult, as past history demonstrates. The old system of sending "advisers" to Liberia whose salaries are charged to the Liberian budget has not produced results, and should not be continued. The "advisers" do not have adequate power and their salaries impose an undue burden on the meager Liberian budget. Some new formula must be found.

Assuming for the moment that a new Liberian reconstruction plan should be American rather than international, it might take the following form:

1. *Improved Diplomatic Representation.* The United States should send an ambassador (not a minister) to Monrovia; and Liberia should send an ambassador to Washington. In the past the diplomatic representative of the United States in Liberia usually has been an American Negro politician, and the result has not been satisfactory. There are able American Negroes who could serve as ambassador, but under the existing system of American politics they are not likely to be appointed. It is to be hoped this situation will soon change. In the immediate future the President of the United States might appoint a high-ranking naval officer as his special representative in Liberia, an appointment justified by the new port and by the precedent of sending Vice Admiral Glassford to Dakar, French West Africa, in May 1943. This special representative should have full power to coordinate any assistance given Liberia by the United States and to see to it that Liberia carries out an agreed reconstruction program. He should remain in Liberia only to initiate the program, being succeeded, say in two years, by an American Negro as Ambassador.

2. *A Twenty-year Agreement Creating Four Joint Commissions.* The United States and Liberia should conclude a twenty-year agreement, approved by our Senate or both Houses of Congress, providing for a Liberian rehabilitation program. This agreement should authorize the construction of the Liberian port.

In the proposed agreement, Liberia and the United States should also undertake to establish joint commissions dealing with economic questions, public health, education, and political affairs. Such commissions should be patterned after similar agencies established elsewhere during World War II, such as the Anglo-American Combined Boards and Chiefs of Staff in Washington, the Middle East Supply Center, and the Anglo-American Caribbean Commission.

The proposed economic, public health and education commissions should have a minimum of three members each: a chairman appointed by the United States and two Liberians appointed by the Liberian Government. The member of the Liberian cabinet dealing with matters entrusted to the joint commission, such as the Secretary of the Treasury in the case of the Economic Commission, might well constitute one of the two Liberian members.

The proposed treaty should provide that if a majority of each commission proposes a given recommendation, the Liberian Government should agree to carry it into effect. Each commission would render periodic reports to the President of Liberia and to the special representative of the President of the United States. The expense of each commission should be divided between the two governments. Instead of saddling the Liberian budget with the cost of the American member, his salary should be borne by the government of the United States.

The Joint Economic Commission could work out a plan for the reorganization of the accounting and tax systems of the government, including the administration of the customs. It should develop a program for Native agriculture and coöperative marketing; it should make a survey of the Native land and labor questions; it should pass upon all applications for foreign concessions. It should make recommendations as to a revision of the Firestone agreements.

The Joint Public Health Commission should continue the work started by the United States Public Health mission. The Joint Education Commission might begin by working out recommendations for the better coördination of American missionary schools in Liberia. Generally, these commissions would do well to study the educational and public health progress in the southern states of the United States and also in adjoining colonies, constantly bearing in mind that the problem of Liberia is not to improve a colony but to strengthen the foundations for independence.

The fourth and most important body would be the Joint Political Commission. Fully recognizing the sensibilities of the Americo-Liberian governing class with respect to questions affecting the political structure and the "sovereignty" of the country, the United States should firmly recognize that no real improvements can be made in Liberia without strengthening and purifying political power. Toward this end a Joint Political Commission should be created, consisting of the President of Liberia as chairman, along with the special representative of the United States and, later, the American ambassador and one other American. Other members should possibly be the Vice-President of Liberia, the Chief Justice of the Supreme Court, a representative of the tribes possibly chosen by a tribal council, and a Liberian not holding any political office. This commission would thus have five Liberian members in contrast to two Americans.

The Liberian Government would not be expected to promise to carry out the recommendations of the majority of the Political Commission, as in the case of the three other joint bodies, since the Political Commission would deal with questions of sovereignty. But by means of such a joint commission, the American representatives could freely express their points of view without having to resort to diplomatic protest and negotiation. The type of question which any member of the Joint Political Commission could raise would be the question of fair elections, the repeal of the Sedition Law, and the need for an improved Native policy. (The improper use of government funds would fall under the jurisdiction of the Joint Economic Commission.) The success of this Commission would depend upon whether the Liberian governing class really desires to improve the country, even at the risk of its political prerogatives, and also upon the tact and strength of the American representatives.

The Joint Commission program can succeed only if it has the support of American Negro opinion. Should the American Negroes attack the program as "imperialism," certainly opposition to the program would be strengthened in Liberia and make it as unworkable as previous programs. American Negro opinion would be pleased if qualified American Negroes should be selected as American representatives on these joint commissions, and where foreign specialists are needed. It is important, however, that the United States avoid the temptation to send to Liberia either white or Negro politicians lacking character or ability. Only the best representation from the United States can insure the success of such a program.

In theory these commissions would be limited to studying problems and making recommendations as to policy. Promising to accept the recommendations of the majority of each of the first three commissions, the Liberian Government would be responsible for the execution of the policy. Some such arrangement is necessary if the Liberian Government is to be strengthened—not weakened—by these new agencies. At the same time, the proper Liberian department could delegate certain specific tasks to the American members of these joint commissions and otherwise make use of their services in the execution of policy.

Sceptics no doubt will predict that this type of program will be no more successful than the American plan of 1921 or the League plan of 1932. They will point out that the joint commissions will not have enough authority to override the opposition of the Liberian Government, and that even though the Government accepts the program at the beginning, it will find means, as in the past, of escaping from its obligations.

While admitting the difficulties involved in reconciling Liberia's independence with foreign assistance, the proposed program would have certain advantages over those hitherto tried. First, Liberians would be associated jointly with Americans on these commissions. They would learn to work together on a basis of equality, which has never been attempted before. Second, the cost of these commissions would not be an exclusive charge on the Liberian Government, nor their chief object to secure payment of the foreign debt. Third, the American representatives would have a higher status on these commissions than past "advisers" have enjoyed. Fourth, the diplomatic representative of the United States would have a position and powers hitherto lacking. The United States would maintain a diplomatic representative on the spot, of much greater prestige than our ministers have hitherto enjoyed, with authority to coordinate the rehabilitation program. If this representative has intelligence, force, and tact, and if he follows the program on a day-by-day basis, the chances are good that the Liberian Government will coöperate. Moreover, the existence of the new port, together with the Firestone plantations and other possible foreign enterprises, inevitably will create a situation where the Liberian Government will have to take more seriously the recommendations of the joint commissions than if no such American interests were in the country. In any case the special representative (and later the United States ambassador) should make it clear that if this plan fails, and if conditions in Liberia again deteriorate, some more drastic action will be demanded not only by American opinion, white and black, but also by Liberia's neighbors.

3. *A United States Government Loan.* Liberians are well-nigh unanimous in opposing new foreign loans from private sources, in view of the unproductive record of such loans in the past and of the profit made from refunding operations by speculators. Undoubtedly, however, they would look with different eyes on a United States Government loan. Such a loan may be necessary to refund the 1926 Firestone obligation so as to get rid of the existing loan officials whose work should be absorbed by the Joint Economic Commission. Such a refunding loan would not enrich speculators because Liberian bonds are not in default, being held entirely by the Finance Corporation of America. Moreover, a United States Government loan would mean cheaper money for the Liberian budget. Any real rehabilitation program will require foreign capital. Such capital could come from a United States Government loan of $5,000,000, which would refund the 1926 loan and yet make available nearly $4,000,000 for productive purposes to be expended only in accordance with the recommendations of the joint commissions. The cost to Liberia of a United States Government loan of $5,000,000 at 2 per cent, the present cost of Government money, would be less than the cost of the Firestone $2,500,000 private loan at 5 per cent. If the American Congress is serious about the assumption of world responsibilities, it should authorize such a loan. For Liberia is our most immediate world responsibility, which hitherto we have neglected. The Firestone Company arranged its loan in 1926 only because the Government was unwilling to revive the 1921 plan. No doubt it would be glad to get rid of its present responsibilities if assured that the Government now had a real program.

4. *A West African Regional Council.* The final question is whether the rehabilitation of Liberia should be an exclusive Liberia-American effort or should take an international form, such as the League Plan of 1932. In view of the uncertain future of international organization, a program of Liberian rehabilitation cannot be entrusted to the United Nations, at least not right away. Nor could this kind of help be expected from the regional councils discussed in England during the war.

In an address to the British Parliament, July 13, 1943, Colonial Secretary Oliver Stanley suggested the creation of regional colonial commissions to develop close coöperation among adjacent colonies, providing permanent machinery for consultation and giving the dependent peoples, as well as governments having economic or strategic interests in the area, a voice in the commissions. A West Africa regional commission would include all the territories from the tiny colony of Rio de Oro in the north (under Spain) to Portuguese Angola in the south. It would thus include the four British West African colonies, French West and Equatorial Africa, the Belgian Congo, and Liberia.[1] This kind of commission, functioning under the aegis of a world organization, could promote both political and social progress.[2]

As proposed, the regional commissions would have only advisory powers, each colonial government being left to apply the suggestions of the regional body. Nevertheless such bodies might grow to the point where they would become kind of a decentralized Mandates Commission but having more influence. The Mandates Commission was limited largely to the negative task of pointing out violation of existing obligations. The regional commissions would have the positive task of making creative suggestions for development. They might propose boundary changes so as to reunite Native tribes now arbitrarily separated by colonial boundary lines; thus the Mende people are divided between Liberia and British Sierra Leone.

The proposed regional commissions could also initiate the negotiation of regional conventions defining minimum social conditions. Such conventions should give the regional commission the power of inspection to see to it that their terms

[1] Joseph M. Jones, "Half of One World," *Fortune,* October 1944.

[2] During the war the British colonies in West Africa made regional progress through a Resident Minister, originally Lord Swinton, who had authority to secure "the effective co-operation in the prosecution of the war of all services, civil and military, throughout West Africa." Once immediate war problems relating to supply, the Naval convoy for the South Atlantic, and other matters were solved, the Minister's office turned to postwar developments. Under the Minister is a Civil Members Committee consisting of the governors of the four British West African colonies and a small secretariat. Some opposition, however, has developed to continuing this regional organization on the ground that it is difficult for a governor to be responsible to a local Minister as well as to the Colonial Office in London. See *African Transcripts,* January 1945, No. I, p. 13; also "West African Regionalism," *The Economist,* December 9, 1944.

are applied.[3] Moreover such a commission could bring about agreement as to the creation of common institutions. As Mr. Henry S. Villard said in his Chautauqua speech, "Africa may require the establishment of an adequate tropical health institute sponsored by governments or by an international organization, to prevent the transmission of disease and to help eradicate local sources of infection." [4]

Valuable as a regional commission might be, the danger is that it would be dominated by the colonial powers, particularly by the least progressive members. In the process of integrating colonies in the same vicinity, the commission might become an instrument for retarding the African demand for self-government. This danger would be reduced if the General Assembly of the new United Nations Organization could elect, say, two members coming from non-colonial powers to this and other regional bodies, and if adequate Negro membership is assured.

Nevertheless it is doubtful whether Liberia would welcome real assistance from a West African regional commission, or whether its participation would be welcomed by the colonial powers. Regarding America as its mother country, Liberia would probably prefer to receive assistance from Washington rather than from a body dominated by colonial powers, just as the Gold Coast or Nigeria would prefer to rely on Great Britain rather than to transfer their dependence to an international body. For a time at least Liberia would be less suspicious of the motives of the United States than of a colonially-minded regional commission. For their part, the colonial governments, and also Native nationalist groups in West Africa, might resent the inclusion of Liberia in a West African regional colonial commission on the ground that Liberia could pass judgment upon conditions in their colonies without having first put its own house in order.

For such reasons it would appear that if the rehabilitation of Liberia is to take place, aid must come direct from the United States in contrast to any regional or international authority.

[3] At the Philadelphia International Labour Office Conference in May 1944, the member states adopted a recommendation concerning minimum standards of social policy in dependent territories. Liberia being a sovereign state, the recommendations do not apply to it as such; but a West African commission (or the United States) could urge Liberia to apply the recommendation by analogy. Liberia ratified the Forced Labor Convention, as part of the reforms made after the slavery exposé of 1931; but it made only two of the annual reports required by the Convention.

[4] *Op. cit.*, p. 724.

Liberia and the United States might submit an annual report to the commission as to the progress of the Liberian rehabilitation program.

If a real United Nations concept is to survive after this war, the United States ought to agree also to open its "military facilities" in Liberia to the forces of any member of the United Nations. By some such means the exclusive position of the United States with respect to Liberia might be made responsible to international authority.

The Liberian Centenary comes in 1947. Already the Monrovia Government has appointed a Centennial Commission, which is working out an elaborate and expensive program. Now there are two ways of celebrating this Centenary. One is merely by eulogizing the Liberian Government and people—and they deserve certain eulogies because of the fact of survival. But eulogies as such will merely cover up deep-seated maladjustments. They must be accompanied by a real rehabilitation program. If the second century of Liberian independence is to be more promising than the first, there is not much time to lose in getting such a program under way.

Appendix 1

FRIENDSHIP, COMMERCE, AND NAVIGATION

Treaty Between the United States and Liberia, Signed at Monrovia, August 8, 1938

Article I

The nationals of each of the High Contracting Parties shall be permitted to enter, travel and reside in the territories of the other; to exercise liberty of conscience and freedom of worship; to engage in professional, scientific, religious, philanthropic, manufacturing and commercial work of every kind without interference; to carry on every form of commercial activity which is not forbidden by the local law; to own, erect or lease and occupy appropriate buildings and to lease lands for residential, scientific, religious, philanthropic, manufacturing, commercial and mortuary purposes; to employ agents of their choice, and generally to do anything incidental to or necessary for the enjoyment of any of the foregoing privileges upon the same terms as nationals of the State of residence or as nationals of the nation hereafter to be most favored by it, submitting themselves to all local laws and regulations duly established.

The nationals of either High Contracting Party within the territories of the other shall not be subjected to the payment of any internal charges or taxes other or higher than those that are exacted of and paid by nationals of the State of residence.

The nationals of each High Contracting Party shall enjoy freedom of access to the courts of justice of the other on conforming to the local laws, as well for the prosecution as for the defense of their rights, and in all degrees of jurisdiction established by law.

The nationals of each High Contracting Party shall receive within the territories of the other, upon submitting to conditions imposed upon its nationals, the most constant protection and security for their persons and property, and shall enjoy in this respect that degree of protection that is required by international law. Their property shall not be taken without due process of law and without payment of just compensation.

Nothing contained in this Treaty shall be construed to affect existing statutes of either of the High Contracting Parties in relation to emigration or to immigration or the right of either of the High Contracting Parties to enact such statutes, provided, however, that nothing in this paragraph shall prevent the nationals of either High Contracting Party from entering, traveling and residing in the territories of the other Party in order to carry on international trade or to engage in any commercial activity related to or connected with the conduct of international trade on the same terms as nationals of the most-favored nation.

ARTICLE II

With respect to that form of protection granted by National, State or Provincial laws establishing civil liability for bodily injuries or for death, and giving to relatives or heirs or dependents of an injured person a right of action or a pecuniary compensation, such relatives or heirs or dependents of the injured person, himself a national of either of the High Contracting Parties and injured within any of the territories of the other, shall, regardless of their alienage or residence outside of the territory where the injury occurred, enjoy the same rights and privileges as are or may be granted to nationals, and under like conditions.

ARTICLE III

The dwellings, warehouses, manufactories, shops, and other places of business, and all premises thereto appertaining of the nationals of each of the High Contracting Parties in the territories of the other, lawfully used for any purposes set forth in Article I, shall be respected. It shall not be allowable to make a domiciliary visit to, or search of any such buildings and premises, or there to examine and inspect books, papers or accounts, except under the conditions and in conformity with the forms prescribed by the laws, ordinances and regulations for nationals of the State of residence or nationals of the nation most favored by it.

ARTICLE IV

Where, on the death of any person holding real or other immovable property or interests therein within the territories of one High Contracting Party, such property or interests therein would, by the laws of the country or by a testamentary disposition, descend or pass to a national of the other High Contracting Party, whether resident or non-resident, were he not disqualified by the laws of the country where such property or interests therein is or are situated, such national shall be allowed a term of three years in which to sell the same, this term to be reasonably prolonged if circumstances render it necessary, and withdraw the proceeds thereof, without restraint or interference and exempt from any estate succession, probate or administrative duties or charges other than those which may be imposed in like cases upon the nationals of the country from which such proceeds may be drawn.

Nationals of either High Contracting Party may have full power to dispose of their personal property of every kind within the territories of the other, by testament, donation, or otherwise, and their heirs, legatees and donees, of whatsoever nationality, whether resident or non-resident, shall succeed to such personal property, and may take possession thereof, either by themselves or by others acting for them, and retain or dispose of the same at their pleasure subject to the payment of such duties or charges only as the nationals of the High Contracting Party within whose territories such property may be or belong shall be liable to pay in like cases. In the same way, personal property left to nationals of one of the High Contracting Parties by nationals of the other High Contracting Party, and being within the territories of such other Party, shall be subject to the payment of such duties or charges only as the nationals of the High Contracting Party within whose territories such property may be or belong shall be liable to pay in like cases.

Article V

The nationals of each of the High Contracting Parties in the exercise of the right of freedom of worship, within the territories of the other, as hereinabove provided, may, without annoyance or molestation of any kind by reason of their religious belief or otherwise, conduct services either within their own houses or within any appropriate buildings which they may be at liberty to erect and maintain in convenient situations, provided their teachings or practices are not contrary to public morals; and they shall also be permitted to bury their dead according to their religious customs in suitable and convenient places established and maintained for the purpose, subject to the mortuary and sanitary laws and regulations of the place of burial.

Article VI

In the event of war between either High Contracting Party and a third State, such Party may draft for compulsory military service nationals of the other having a permanent residence within its territories and who have formally, according to its laws, declared an intention to adopt its nationality by naturalization, unless such persons depart from the territories of said belligerent Party within sixty days after the declaration of war. Such right to depart shall apply also to persons possessing the nationality of both High Contracting Parties unless they habitually reside in the territory of the country drafting for compulsory military service.

It is agreed, however, that such right to depart shall not apply to natives of the country drafting for compulsory military service, who, after having become nationals of the other Party, have declared an intention to acquire or resume the nationality of the country of their birth. Such persons shall nevertheless be entitled in respect of this matter to treatment no less favorable than that accorded the nationals of any other country who are similarly situated.

Article VII

Between the territories of the High Contracting Parties there shall be freedom of commerce and navigation. The nationals of each of the High Contracting Parties equally with those of the most-favored nation, shall have liberty freely to come with their vessels and cargoes to all places, ports and waters of every kind within the territorial limits of the other which are or may be open to foreign commerce and navigation.

Article VIII

With respect to customs duties or charges of any kind imposed on or in connection with importation or exportation, and with respect to the method of levying such duties or charges, and with respect to all rules and formalities in connection with importation or exportation, and with respect to all laws or regulations affecting the sale, taxation, or use of imported goods within the country, any advantage, favor, privilege or immunity which has been or may hereafter be granted by either High Contracting Party to any article originating in or destined for any third country, shall be accorded immediately and unconditionally to the like article originating in or destined for the other High Contracting Party.

With respect to the amount and collection of duties on imports and exports of every kind, each of the two High Contracting Parties binds itself to give to the nationals, vessels and goods of the other the advantage of every favor, privilege or immunity which it shall have accorded to the nationals, vessels and goods of a third State, whether such favored State shall have been accorded such treatment gratuitously or in return for reciprocal compensatory treatment. Every such favor, privilege or immunity which shall hereafter be granted to nationals, vessels or goods of a third State shall simultaneously and unconditionally, without request and without compensation, be extended to the other High Contracting Party, for the benefit of itself, its nationals, vessels, and goods.

Article IX

Neither of the High Contracting Parties shall establish or maintain any import or export prohibition or restriction on any article originating in or destined for the territory of the other High Contracting Party, which is not applied to the like article originating in or destined for any third country. Any abolition of an import or export prohibition or restriction which may be granted even temporarily by either High Contracting Party in favor of an article originating in or destined for a third country shall be applied immediately and unconditionally to the like article originating in or destined for the territory of the other High Contracting Party.

If either High Contracting Party establishes or maintains any form of quantitative restriction or control of the importation or sale of any article in which the other High Contracting Party has an interest, or imposes a lower import duty or charge on the importation or sale of a specified quantity of any such article than the duty or charge imposed on importations in excess of such quantity, the High Contracting Party taking such action shall, upon request, inform the other High Contracting Party as to the total quantity, or any change therein, of any such article permitted to be imported or sold, or permitted to be imported or sold at such lower duty or charge during a specified period, and shall allot to the other High Contracting Party for such specified period a proportion of such total quantity as originally established or subsequently changed in any manner equivalent to the proportion of the total importation of such article which the other High Contracting Party supplied during a previous representative period, unless it is mutually agreed to dispense with such allotment. Neither of the High Contracting Parties shall, by import licenses, regulate the total quantity of importations into its territory or sales therein of any article in which the other High Contracting Party has an interest, unless the total quantity of such article permitted to be imported or sold during a quota period of not less than three months shall have been established, and unless the regulations covering the issuance of such licenses or permits shall have been made public before such regulations are put into force.

Article X

If either High Contracting Party establishes or maintains, directly or indirectly, any form of control of the means of international payment, it shall, in the administration of such control:

(a) Impose no prohibition, restriction, or delay on the transfer of payment for imported articles the growth, produce, or manufacture of the other High Contracting Party, or of payments necessary for and incidental to the importation of such articles;

(b) Accord unconditionally, with respect to rates of exchange and taxes or surcharges on exchange transactions in connection with payments for or payments necessary and incidental to the importation of articles the growth, produce, or manufacture of the other High Contracting Party, treatment no less favorable than that accorded in connection with the importation of any article whatsoever the growth, produce, or manufacture of any third country; and

(c) Accord unconditionally, with respect to all rules and formalities applying to exchange transactions in connection with payments for or payments necessary and incidental to the importation of articles the growth, produce, or manufacture of the other High Contracting Party, treatment no less favorable than that accorded in connection with the importation of the like articles the growth, produce, or manufacture of any third country.

With respect to non-commercial transactions, each High Contracting Party shall apply any form of control of the means of international payment in a non-discriminatory manner as between the nationals of the other High Contracting Party and the nationals of any third country.

ARTICLE XI

In the event that either High Contracting Party establishes or maintains a monopoly for the importation, production or sale of a particular product or grants exclusive privileges, formally or in effect, to one or more agencies to import, produce or sell a particular product, the High Contracting Party establishing or maintaining such monopoly, or granting such monopoly privileges, shall, in respect of the foreign purchases of such monopoly or agency, accord the commerce of the other High Contracting Party fair and equitable treatment. In making its foreign purchases of any article such monopoly or agency shall be influenced solely by competitive considerations such as price, quality, marketability, and terms of sale.

ARTICLE XII

All articles which are or may be legally imported from foreign countries into ports of the United States of America or are or may be legally exported therefrom in vessels of the United States may likewise be imported into those ports or exported therefrom in Liberian vessels, without being liable to any other or higher duties or charges whatsoever than if such articles were imported or exported in vessels of the United States; and reciprocally, all articles which are or may be legally imported from foreign countries into the ports of Liberia or are or may be legally exported therefrom in Liberian vessels may likewise be imported into those ports or exported therefrom in vessels of the United States without being liable to any other or higher duties or charges whatsoever than if such articles were imported or exported in Liberian vessels.

In the same manner there shall be perfect reciprocal equality in relation to the flags of the two countries with regard to bounties, drawbacks, and other privileges of this nature of whatever denomination which may be allowed in the territories of each of the Contracting Parties, on goods imported or exported in national vessels so that such bounties, drawbacks and other privileges shall also and in like manner be allowed on goods imported or exported in vessels of the other country.

ARTICLE XIII

The nationals, goods, products, wares, and merchandise of each High Contracting Party within the territories of the other shall receive the same treatment as nationals, goods, products, wares, and merchandise of the country with regard to internal taxes, transit duties, charges in respect of warehousing and other facilities and the amount of drawbacks and export bounties.

Article XIV

The merchant or other private vessels and cargoes of one of the High Contracting Parties shall, within the territorial waters and harbors of the other Party in all respects and unconditionally be accorded the same treatment as the vessel and cargoes of that Party, irrespective of the port of departure of the vessel, or the port of destination, and irrespective of the origin or the destination of the cargo. It is especially agreed that no duties of tonnage, harbor, pilotage, lighthouse, quarantine, or other similar or corresponding duties or charges of whatever denomination, levied in the name or for the profit of the Government, public functionaries, private individuals, corporations or establishments of any kind shall be imposed in the ports of the territories or territorial waters of either country upon the vessels of the other, which shall not equally, under the same conditions, be imposed on national vessels.

Article XV

Merchant vessels and other privately owned vessels under the flag of either of the High Contracting Parties, and carrying the papers required by its national laws in proof of nationality shall, both within the territorial waters of the other High Contracting Party and on the high seas, be deemed to be the vessels of the Party whose flag is flown.

Article XVI

Merchant vessels and other privately owned vessels under the flag of either of the High Contracting Parties shall be permitted to discharge portions of cargoes at any port open to foreign commerce in the territories of the other High Contracting Party, and to proceed with the remaining portions of such cargoes to any other ports of the same territories open to foreign commerce, without paying other or higher tonnage dues or port charges in such cases than would be paid by national vessels in like circumstances, and they shall be permitted to load in like manner at different ports in the same voyage outward, provided, however, that the coasting trade of the High Contracting Parties is exempt from the provisions of this Article and from the other provisions of this Treaty, and is to be regulated according to the laws of each High Contracting Party in relation thereto. It is agreed, however, that nationals and vessels of either High Contracting Party shall within the territories of the other enjoy with respect to the coasting trade most-favored-nation treatment.

Article XVII

Limited liability and other corporations and associations, whether or not for pecuniary profit, which have been or may hereafter be organized in accordance with and under the laws, National, State or Provincial, of either High Contracting Party and which maintain a central office within the territories thereof, shall have their juridical status recognized by the other High Contracting Party provided that they pursue no aims within its territories contrary to its laws. They shall enjoy free access to the courts of law and equity, on conforming to the laws regulating the matter, as well for the prosecution as for the defense of rights in all the degrees of jurisdiction established by law.

The right of corporations and associations of either High Contracting Party which have been so recognized by the other to establish themselves in the territories of the other Party or to establish branch offices and fulfill their functions therein shall depend upon and be governed solely by the consent of such Party as expressed in its National, State or Provincial laws.

Article XVIII

The nationals of either High Contracting Party shall enjoy within the territories of the other, upon compliance with the conditions there imposed, such rights and privileges as have been or may hereafter be accorded the nationals of any other State with respect to organization of and participation in limited liability and other corporations and associations, for pecuniary profit or otherwise, including the rights of promotion, incorporation, purchase and ownership and sale of shares and the holding of executive or official positions therein. In the exercise of the foregoing rights and with respect to the regulation or procedure concerning the organization or conduct of such corporations or associations, such nationals shall be subjected to no condition less favorable than those which have been or may hereafter be imposed upon the nationals of the most-favored nation. The right of any of such corporations or associations as may be organized or controlled or participated in by the nationals of either High Contracting Party within the territories of the other to exercise any of their functions therein, shall be governed by the laws and regulations, National, State or Provincial, which are in force or may hereafter be established within the territories of the Party wherein they propose to carry on their activities. The foregoing stipulations do not apply to organization of and participation in political associations.

Article XIX

The nationals, including corporations and associations, of either High Contracting Party shall enjoy in the territories of the other Party, upon compliance with the conditions there imposed, most-favored-nation treatment in respect of the exploration for and exploitation of mineral resources; provided that neither Party shall be required to grant rights and privileges in respect of the mining of coal, phosphate, oil, oil shale, gas and sodium on the public domain, or in respect of the ownership of stock in domestic corporations engaged in such operations, greater than its nationals, corporations and associations receive from the other Party.

It is understood, however, that neither High Contracting Party shall be required by anything in this paragraph to grant any application for any such right or privilege if at the time such application is presented the granting of all similar applications shall have been suspended or discontinued.

Article XX

Commercial travelers representing manufacturers, merchants and traders domiciled in the territories of either High Contracting Party shall on their entry into and sojourn in the territories of the other Party and on their departure therefrom be accorded the most-favored-nation treatment in respect of customs and other privileges and of all charges and taxes of whatever denomination applicable to them or to their samples.

If either High Contracting Party requires the presentation of an authentic document establishing the identity and authority of a commercial traveler, a signed statement by the concern or concerns represented, certified by a consular officer of the country of destination shall be accepted as satisfactory.

Article XXI

There shall be complete freedom of transit through the territories including territorial waters of each High Contracting

Party on the routes most convenient for international transit, by rail, navigable waterway, and canal, other than the Panama Canal and waterways and canals which constitute international boundaries, to persons and goods coming from, going to or passing through the territories of the other High Contracting Party, except such persons as may be forbidden admission into its territories or goods of which the importation may be prohibited by law or regulations, provided that the foregoing shall not be construed to prevent either High Contracting Party from excluding aliens from special areas within its territories closed to visit by law, military order or regulations. The measures of a general or particular character which either of the High Contracting Parties is obliged to take in case of an emergency affecting the safety of the State or vital interests of the country may, in exceptional cases and for as short a period as possible, involve a deviation from the provisions of this paragraph, it being understood that the principle of freedom of transit must be observed to the utmost possible extent.

Persons and goods in transit shall not be subjected to any transit duty, or to any unnecessary delays or restrictions, or to treatment as regards charges, facilities, or any other matter less favorable than that accorded to the most-favored nation.

Goods in transit must be entered at the proper customhouse, but they shall be exempt from all customs or other similar duties.

It is understood that all goods in transit through the territory of the United States of America and all goods in transit through the territory of Liberia when warehoused or otherwise stored shall be subject to storage charges.

All charges imposed on transport in transit shall be reasonable, having regard to the conditions of the traffic.

Nothing in this Article shall affect the right of either of the High Contracting Parties to prohibit or restrict the transit of arms, munitions and military equipment in accordance with treaties or conventions that may have been or may hereafter be entered into by either Party with other countries.

Article XXII

Nothing in this Treaty shall be construed to prevent the adoption of measures prohibiting or restricting the exportation or importation of gold or silver, or to prevent the adoption of such measures as either High Contracting Party may see fit with respect to the prohibition, or the control, of the export or sale for export, of arms, ammunition, or implements of war, and, in exceptional circumstances, all other military supplies.

Subject to the requirement that, under like circumstances and conditions, there shall be no arbitrary discrimination by either High Contracting Party against the other High Contracting Party in favor of any third country, the stipulations of this Treaty shall not extend to prohibitions or restrictions (1) imposed on moral or humanitarian grounds; (2) designed to protect human, animal, or plant life or health; (3) relating to prison-made goods; (4) relating to the enforcement of police or revenue laws.

The stipulations of this Treaty do not extend to advantages now accorded or which may hereafter be accorded to neighboring States in order to facilitate short frontier traffic, or to advantages resulting from a customs union to which either High Contracting Party may become a party so long as such advantages are not extended to any other country.

The stipulations of this Treaty do not extend to advantages now accorded or which may hereafter be accorded by the United States of America, its territories or possessions or the Panama Canal Zone to one another or to the Republic of Cuba. The provisions of this paragraph shall continue to apply in respect of any advantages now or hereafter accorded by the United States of America, its territories or possessions or the Panama Canal Zone to one another, irrespective of any change in the political status of any of the territories or possessions of the United States of America.

Article XXIII

Subject to any limitation or exception hereinabove set forth, or hereafter to be agreed upon the territories of the High Contracting Parties to which the provisions of this Treaty extend shall be understood to comprise all areas of land and water over which the Parties, respectively, claim and exercise dominion as sovereign thereof, except the Panama Canal Zone.

Article XXIV

The present Treaty shall come into force in all of its provisions on the day of the exchange of ratifications and shall continue in force for the term of five years from that day.

If within one year before the expiration of five years from the date on which the present Treaty shall come into force, neither

High Contracting Party notifies to the other Party an intention of terminating the Treaty upon the expiration of the aforesaid period of five years, the Treaty shall remain in full force and effect after the aforesaid period and until one year from such a time as either of the High Contracting Parties shall have notified to the other Party an intention of terminating it.

The present Treaty shall, from the date of the exchange of ratifications, be deemed to supplant the Treaty of Commerce and Navigation between the United States of America and Liberia, concluded at London on October 21, 1862.

Article XXV

The present Treaty shall be ratified, and the ratifications thereof shall be exchanged at Monrovia as soon as possible.

In witness whereof the respective Plenipotentiaries have signed the present Treaty and have affixed their seals thereto.

Done in duplicate, at Monrovia, this eighth day of August nineteen hundred and thirty eight.

[SEAL] Lester A. Walton
[SEAL] C. L. Simpson

Appendix 2

DEFENSE AREAS

Agreement Between the United States and Liberia, Signed at Monrovia, March 31, 1942

ARTICLE 1

The grants of rights specified above [in the preamble] shall also include the right to improve and deepen channels, to construct connecting roads, communication services, fortifications, repair and storage facilities and housing for personnel, and generally the right to do any and all things necessary to insure the efficient operation, maintenance and protection of such defense facilities as may be established;

ARTICLE 2

The Republic of Liberia retains sovereignty over all such airports, fortifications and other defense areas as may be established under the rights above granted. The Government of the United States during the life of this Agreement shall have exclusive jurisdiction over any such airports and defense areas in Liberia and over the military and civilian personnel of the Government of the United States and their families within the airports, fortifications and other defense areas, as well as over all other persons within such areas except Liberian citizens.

It is understood, however, that the Government of the United States may turn over to the Liberian authorities for trial and punishment any person committing an offense in such defense areas. And the Liberian authorities will turn over to the United States authorities for trial and punishment any of the United States military or civilian personnel and their families who may commit offenses outside such defense areas. The Liberian authorities and the United States authorities will take adequate measure to insure the prosecution and punishment in cases of conviction of all such offenders, it being understood that the relevant evidence shall be furnished reciprocally to the two authorities.

Article 3

It is agreed that the Government of the United States shall have the right to establish and maintain postal facilities and commissary stores to be used solely by the military and civilian personnel of the United States Government and their families stationed in Liberia in connection with this Agreement and with such aid in the defense of Liberia as the Government of the United States may furnish.

Article 4

All materials, supplies and equipment for the construction, use and operation of said airports of the United States Government and for the personal needs of the military and civilian personnel and their families, shall be permitted entry into Liberia free of customs duties, excise taxes, or any other charges, and the said personnel and their families shall also be exempt from all forms of taxes, assessments, and other levies by the Liberian Government and authorities, including exemption from Liberian regulations pertaining to passports, visas and residence permits.

The Government of the United States undertakes to respect all legitimate interests of Liberia and Liberian citizens, as well as all the laws, regulations and customs relating to the native population and the internal administration of Liberia. In exercising the rights derived from this Agreement, the Government of the United States undertakes to give sympathetic consideration to all representations made by the Liberian authorities with respect to the welfare of the inhabitants of Liberia.

In respect of the commercial use of such airports, passengers, mail and cargo entering or leaving Liberia by air shall have transit over such airports to and from a Liberian customs station established adjacent to said airports and under the exclusive jurisdiction of the Government of Liberia.

Article 5

The Government of the United States undertakes to extend to the Government of Liberia such aid as may be possible in the circumstances in the protection of the Republic, including necessary equipment for road construction, certain monetary aids for defense purposes, certain assistance in the organization and training of the Liberian military forces and certain other assistance of a similar nature.

Article 6

The Government of the United States undertakes, at the end of the war and the additional period provided in Paragraph 5 of the Preamble to this Agreement, to withdraw all military forces of the United States. It is mutually understood and agreed that the jurisdiction hereby conferred on the Government of the United States over any airports and defense areas, and over military and civilian personnel under the provisions of Article 2 of this Agreement, shall continue until all matters calling for judicial determination, but undisposed of after the termination of this Agreement, shall have been disposed of by the United States authorities, or, alternately, until the withdrawal of the United States forces shall be complete.

Article 7

The Government of Liberia and the Government of the United States agree that at this time the above Agreement shall apply to the air facilities at Roberts Field on the Farmington River, and at Fisherman Lake in the County of Grand Cape Mount. If other defense areas of this kind are deemed necessary in the future, their location will be fixed by mutual agreement.

Article 8

For the purposes of this Agreement, a Defense Area shall be construed as the actual areas of said airports and such additional areas in the immediate neighborhood upon which installations necessary for defense may be established by the agreement between the United States Commanding Officer and the Liberian Government.

Appendix 3

PRINCIPLES APPLYING TO MUTUAL AID FOR DEFENSE

Agreement Between the United States and Liberia, Signed at New York, June 8, 1943

ARTICLE I

The Government of the United States of America will continue to supply the Government of the Republic of Liberia with such defense articles, defense services, and defense information as the President of the United States of America shall authorize to be transferred or provided.

ARTICLE II

The Government of the Republic of Liberia will provide to the Government of the United States of America such articles, services, facilities or information as it may be in a position to supply.

ARTICLE III

The Government of the Republic of Liberia will not without the consent of the President of the United States of America transfer title to, or possession of, any defense article or defense information transferred to it under the Act of March 11, 1941 of the Congress of the United States of America or permit the use thereof by anyone not an officer, employee, or agent of the Government of the Republic of Liberia.

ARTICLE IV

If, as a result of the transfer to the Government of the Republic of Liberia of any defense article or defense information, it becomes necessary for that Government to take any action or make any payment in order fully to protect any of the rights of a citizen of the United States of America who has patent rights in and to any such defense article or information, the Government of the Republic of Liberia will take such action or make such payment when requested to do so by the President of the United States of America.

ARTICLE V

The Government of the Republic of Liberia will return to the United States of America at the end of the present emergency, as determined by the President of the United States of America, such defense articles transferred under this Agreement as shall not have been destroyed, lost or consumed and as shall be determined by him to be useful in the defense of the United States of America or of the Western Hemisphere or to be otherwise of use to the United States of America.

ARTICLE VI

In the final determination of the benefits to be provided to the United States of America by the Government of the Republic of Liberia full cognizance shall be taken of all property, services, information, facilities, or other benefits or considerations provided by the Government of the Republic of Liberia subsequent to March 11, 1941, and accepted or acknowledged by the President on behalf of the United States of America.

ARTICLE VII

In the final determination of the benefits to be provided to the United States of America by the Government of the Republic of Liberia in return for aid furnished under the Act of Congress of March 11, 1941, the terms and conditions thereof shall be such as not to burden commerce between the two countries, but to promote mutually advantageous economic relations between them and the betterment of world-wide economic relations. To that end, they shall include provision for agreed action by the United States of America and the Republic of Liberia, open to participation by all other countries of like mind, directed to the expansion, by appropriate international and domestic measures, of production, employment, and the exchange and consumption of goods, which are the material foundations of the liberty and welfare of all peoples; to the elimination of all forms of discriminatory treatment in international commerce; to the reduction of tariffs and other trade barriers; and, in general, to the attainment of all the economic objectives set forth in the Joint Declaration made on August

14, 1941, by the President of the United States of America and the Prime Minister of the United Kingdom, known as the Atlantic Charter.

At an early convenient date, conversations shall be begun between the two Governments with a view to determining, in the light of governing economic conditions, the best means of attaining the above-stated objectives by their own agreed action and of seeking the agreed action of other like-minded Governments.

Article VIII

This Agreement shall take effect as from this day's date. It shall continue in force until a date to be agreed upon by the two Governments.

Signed and sealed in the city of New York in duplicate this eighth day of June 1943.

Appendix 4

CONSTRUCTION OF A PORT AND PORT WORKS

Agreement Between the United States and Liberia, Signed at Monrovia, December 31, 1943

ARTICLE 1

The Government of the United States of America will make available to the Government of the Republic of Liberia under the terms of the Mutual Aid Agreement of June 8, 1943, such funds as may be allotted by the administrative agency of the Government of the United States of America which is or may be authorized and empowered to administer the provisions of the Act of Congress of the United States of America approved March 11, 1941, in the form of a credit under conditions to be determined by such administrative agency, for the surveying of the estuary of the St. Paul River and such other sites in the vicinity of Monrovia and Marshall as may be necessary for the satisfactory location of the port, and for the construction of a port and port works and access roads at the estuary of the St. Paul River or at such other site in the vicinity of Monrovia or Marshall as may be eventually preferred by the Government of the United States of America and the Government of the Republic of Liberia.

ARTICLE 2

The Government of the Republic of Liberia will enter into a contract with an American company, duly incorporated in the United States of America and approved by the Government of the United States of America for the effectuation of the necessary survey, or surveys, and the construction of the port and port works and access roads, which American company, upon preparing its plans and estimates, shall submit said plans and estimates to the Government of the United States of America and to the Government of the Republic of Liberia for approval.

ARTICLE 3

The Government of the Republic of Liberia agrees to the establishment of the port as a free port, or foreign trade zone, to be operated for the mutual benefit of the United States of America and the Republic of Liberia and all nations with which the United States of America and the Republic of Liberia maintain friendly relations, under such conditions and by such means as may henceforth be provided. The Government of the Republic of Liberia undertakes to make available, without cost, to the operating company provided for in Article 5, such land and rights in land as may be necessary for the construction of the free port and such land and rights in land contiguous to the port site as may be necessary for the efficient operation, maintenance and protection of the free port.

ARTICLE 4

Upon approval of the plans and estimates, as prescribed in Article 2, the contracting company shall, with the assent of the administrative agency of the Government of the United States of America which is or may be authorized and empowered to administer the provisions of the Act of the Congress of the United States of America approved March 11, 1941, proceed with the construction of the port and port works and access roads as soon as practicable, under the direction of American engineers.

ARTICLE 5

Prior to the construction of the port and port works and access roads, a contract shall be entered into between the Government of the Republic of Liberia and an American company, duly incorporated in the United States of America or in the Republic of Liberia and approved by the Government of the United States of America, for the operation of the port during the full period of amortization, as shall be hereinafter provided, commencing from the date of completion of the port and port works and access roads or from such earlier date as the port is able to begin receiving ships and cargo. The said contract shall provide for adequate and equitable representation by the Government of the Republic of Liberia on any Board of Directors or Port Authority which may be set up for the operation of the port.

Provision shall be made in the aforesaid contract for the payment, from revenues of the port, of the administrative and other costs of operating the port and for annual payments in amortization of the funds made available by the Government of the United States of America for the construction of the port and port works and access roads, excluding any installations which may be constructed under Article 7 of this Agreement. Such annual payments shall be paid by the operating company to the Government of the Republic of Liberia for transmission to the Government of the United States of America and shall be computed on the basis of such agreed percentage of the net revenues of the port as may be specified in the aforesaid contract. The aforesaid contract shall also provide for such increases in the percentage of amortization payments as may be subsequently determined upon from time to time by the operating company and the Government of the Republic of Liberia, subject to the approval of the Government of the United States of America.

In the event of reasonable complaint by the Government of the Republic of Liberia upon due cause shown, regarding improper or inefficient performance in the operation of the port on the part of the operating company, the Government of the United States of America undertakes to receive and afford full consideration to such complaint, and reserves the right, in agreement with the Government of the Republic of Liberia, to withdraw its approval of the said contract on giving one year's notice to the operating company and to authorize transference of operating control to such other American company as may be agreed upon between the Government of the United States of America and the Government of the Republic of Liberia.

Article 6

When amortization of the cost of the port, port works and access roads shall have been fully completed, operating control and ownership of all installations constructed from funds made available by the Government of the United States of America under the Mutual Aid Agreement of June 8, 1943, shall pass to the Government of the Republic of Liberia. If, however, any such installations as are provided for in Article 7 of this Agreement have been actually completed or undertaken by the Government of the United States of America at the time of such full amortization, the Government of the United States of America and the Government of the Republic of Liberia agree to consider jointly the future terms and manner of operation of the port under the control of a Port Authority which shall be constituted in a form mutually satisfactory to the two Governments and which shall operate in consonance with the stipulations of Article 7 of this Agreement.

Article 7

The Government of the Republic of Liberia, upon request, will grant to the Government of the United States of America the right to establish, use, maintain, improve, supplement, guard and control, in part or their entirety, at the expense of the Government of the United States of America, such naval, air and military facilities and installations at the site of the port, and in the general vicinity thereof, as may be desired by the Government of the United States of America for the protection of the strategic interests of the United States of America in the South Atlantic.

The Government of the United States of America undertakes to respect, in the future as in the past, the territorial integrity, sovereignty, and political independence of the Republic of Liberia.

Article 8

The Government of the United States of America shall be exempt from the payment of Liberian taxes of any kind in connection with the construction, operation or maintenance of its naval, air and military facilities and installations under this Agreement.

Article 9

This Agreement shall take effect on the date of signature.

Signed and sealed in Monrovia in duplicate this thirty-first day of December 1943.

Appendix 5

THE PLANTING AGREEMENT OF 1926

Between Liberia and the Firestone Plantation Company, with amendments of 1935, 1936, 1937, and 1939

Article I

That the Government hath agreed and by these presents doth agree to grant, demise and to farm-let unto the Lessee for the period of Ninety-nine years from this date an area of land within the boundaries of the Republic of Liberia of one million acres or any lesser area that may be selected by the Lessee from time to time within said period of Ninety-nine years; such land to be suitable for the production of rubber or other agricultural products.

But should the Lessee fail

(a) To notify the Government of its acceptance of the conditions herein contained and stipulated within six months after the execution of this Agreement by the Government of Liberia;

(b) Or within one year thereafter to commence the selection of lands hereunder;

Then in such case the obligation of the Government under this Agreement shall be discharged and ended.

The Government, in consideration (1) of the establishment of Lessee's enterprise in the Republic of Liberia, (2) the payment of the revenue tax for which provision is made in paragraph (d) of Article III hereof, (3) the prepayment by Lessee of the sum of Four Hundred Thousand ($400,000) dollars in bonds, at par, of the Liberian Government issued under the Loan Agreement of 1926, or any amendment thereof, as rent in full upon the one hundred and ten thousand (110,000) acres, approximately, of land now held by it under the Planting Agreement and the lease dated March 1, 1935, for the 90-year period beginning October 2, 1935, and ending October 2, 2025, and (4) the further payment of the sum of Two Hundred and Fifty Thousand ($250,000) dollars in such bonds, at par, agrees that during the life of this Agreement Lessee shall have and enjoy the following additional rights and exemptions: [1]

(a) The Lessee shall be entitled to make such importations as it shall deem necessary for the operation and development of its plantations and to export without restriction the products thereof and freely to transport such exports and imports by land or water within the Republic; and the Lessee, except with respect to documentary stamp taxes of general application not exceeding existing rates as applied to exports and imports, shall be wholly free and exempt from any and all taxes, duties, dues, imposts, excises, license fees, inspection fees, wharfage dues, harbour dues, highways tolls, and all other charges of whatsoever sort, description, or designation now or hereafter authorized, levied, or imposed by the Republic of Liberia or by any entity now or hereafter acting or existing by its authority in the exercise of the inherent or delegated power (1) to tax persons, tangible or intangible property, transactions, or occupations; (2) to lay duties upon exports and imports or either; or (3) to subject the exercise of any lawful activity to the payment of license fees, inspection fees, wharfage or harbour dues, highway tolls or any other imposition whatsoever, whether of the general character of those herein expressly mentioned or otherwise; provided, nevertheless, that the exemptions from import and export duties hereby granted shall be and are restricted to the importation of things and substances for use, directly or indirectly, by the Lessee upon its leased lands in the operation and development thereof and not for sale or barter and to the exportation of the products of Lessee's leased lands; and provided further that motor vehicles in excess of one hundred and fifty owned and operated at any one time by Lessee shall be subject to the same license fees and taxes as are similar vehicles owned and/or operated by others.[2]

(b) The Lessee's foreign employees, under contract or otherwise, shall be permitted to reside and work in the Republic, and to enter and depart therefrom, and they shall not be subject to the payment of any direct or personal taxes of whatsoever character; provided, nevertheless, that nothing herein contained shall be construed as creating an exemption in favor of such employees with respect to general property taxes or customs duties.[3]

[1] Amendment of March 20, 1935, Annex B.
[2] Amendment of March 20, 1935, Annex B.
[3] Amendment of March 20, 1935, Annex B.

(c) Lessee shall have the exclusive right and privilege upon the lands which shall be selected under this Agreement to construct highways, railways and waterways for the efficient operation and development of the properties. It is agreed that all trails across such lands used immemorially by the population shall be subject and open to free use by the public.

(d) Lessee shall have the right to construct and establish, at its own expense, lines of communication and transportation such as highways, roadways, waterways, power lines, pipe lines and railways outside the lands selected under this Agreement. Such routes may be so located by the Lessee as to best serve the purpose of efficient operation of its plantations and enterprises, but the Lessee agrees to consult the Government in the matter of such location. All highways and roadways in this paragraph mentioned shall, upon completion, become public property. But the Government, in any event, shall not be required to refund to the Lessee any sums of money expended by it in the construction and maintenance of such highways, roadways, waterways or railways.

Lessee may use during the term of this Agreement any Government land not already devoted to some other incompatible use, for rights of way, not to exceed eighty (80) feet in width and station areas not exceeding five acres, for any highway, roadway, waterway, power line, pipe line or railway constructed by it beyond the confines of land held by it under lease by selection under this Agreement; provided, that for lands occupied by the Lessee under the provisions of this paragraph, rent shall be paid at the rate provided by Paragraph (c) of Article III hereof except as to such land situated within the boundaries of organized municipalities, as to which land rent shall be paid at the rate of 50¢ per acre per annum.[4]

(e) The Lessee shall have the right to construct, maintain and operate lines of communication for the purpose of more efficiently operating its plantations and enterprises, such as telegraph lines, telephone lines and radio communication stations upon the lands selected and held under this Agreement and beyond the confines thereof, subject to the provisions of paragraph (h), Article IV of this Agreement. To the extent necessary for any or all of the foregoing purposes, the Lessee may use, for a period to expire with this Agreement, any Government land not already devoted to some other incompatible use, pro-

[4] Amendment of December 28, 1939, Annex I.

vided that the width of any right of way so occupied on Government land for telegraph or telephone lines shall not exceed forty (40) feet, and that land, occupied exclusively for telegraph, telephone or radio stations shall not exceed five acres in extent. The Lessee shall also be and is hereby granted the right, directly or through any corporate subsidiaries or affiliates, as licensees or assignees, to construct, maintain and operate for its own use and that of its subsidiary or affiliate corporations and for public service a domestic and foreign radio communication system; and to determine the rates to be charged the public for such service; provided, however, that the Government shall be entitled to transmit messages on official business over any radio system established hereunder at rates not exceeding one half of the rates charged the general public; and provided, further, that the rates charged the public for domestic service shall be fixed by agreement with the Government and the rates for foreign service shall not be higher than those charged by any competing radio service; and provided further, that messages deposited by the public, with any Government radio station now or hereafter existing for transmission on the domestic or foreign radio communication system of the Lessee established hereunder shall be transmitted by radio communication by said Government radio station to the nearest radio receiving station of the Lessee according to the rates, schedules and conditions to be fixed by Agreement with the Government. All tax exemptions granted the Lessee under the provisions of paragraph (a) of Article II of this Agreement or any amendment thereof shall be enjoyed by any subsidiary or affiliate corporation operating a radio service under license or assignment by Lessee of the rights granted by this paragraph. The frequencies granted the Lessee by its contract with the Government of the Republic of Liberia dated January 22, 1929, and now in use under assignment by its subsidiary United States Liberia Radio Corporation, and the frequencies enumerated in the letter of the Firestone Plantations Company to the Postmaster General of the Republic of Liberia, dated February 9, 1934, and as set out in the Memorandum of Agreement between the Lessee and the Postmaster General of the Republic of Liberia, dated March 20th, 1935, together with frequencies 35140, 33860, 37060 and 37460 for point to point radio communication between the Lessee's stations in Liberia, shall be available to the Lessee and/or its subsidiaries, affiliates, licensees, or assignees during the life of this Agreement. The Government in case of war or other public emergency, so declared by the President of Liberia, shall have the right to use the lines of communication to which this paragraph relates.[5]

(f) The Lessee shall have the right to cut and use all timber upon the lands covered by this Agreement but if it shall engage in the sale of lumber to be removed from such lands for export it shall pay the Government royalty of two (2) cents per cubic foot for the lumber so sold.[6]

(g) The Lessee shall have the exclusive right to engage in any operations upon the lands held under this Agreement in addition to the agricultural activities herein authorized, including the exclusive right to take by mining or any similar operations the mineral contents of the subsoil of the leased lands; provided, nevertheless, that any previous metals or precious stones so obtained by Lessee shall be subject to a royalty payment to the Government of not to exceed ten per centum (10%) of the value thereof.[7]

(h) The Government warrants to the Lessee the title to all lands selected by it upon which the Government shall accept the rental or compensation as herein provided and will defend and protect such title for the benefit of the Lessee.

The Government further agrees that it will encourage, support and assist the efforts of the Lessee to secure and maintain an adequate labour supply, and to that end the Lessee shall not be required by compulsion of law to maintain a scale of wages, benefits and conditions of employment in excess of (1) the average of the prevailing compensation paid (2) benefits granted and (3) conditions of employment maintained from time to time by other employers of like labour in comparable work for like hours of labor in Liberia and other tropical countries of West Africa.[8]

Article III

The Lessee in consideration of the Agreements herein by the Government hath agreed and by these presents doth agree as follows:

(a) To notify the Government within a period of six (6) months after the execution of this Agreement by the Govern-

[5] Amendment of March 20, 1935 as further amended by the Agreement of December 28, 1939, Annex I. New matter introduced by the latter amendment.

[6] Amendment of March 3, 1936, Annex F.

[7] Amendment of March 20, 1935, Annex B.

[8] Amendment of November 10, 1937, Annex G.

ment of Liberia of its acceptance or rejection of the conditions and stipulations of this Agreement.

(b) Beginning one year after the acceptance by the Lessee of this Agreement it shall select from year to year land suitable for the production of rubber and other agricultural products in such areas or quantities within the maximum limit of one million acres of land as may be convenient to it and in accordance with the economical and progressive development of its holdings; and said Lessee shall upon the selection or location of any tract or tracts of land notify the Government of such selection and the boundaries thereof. But the Lessee shall within five years of the final execution of this Agreement select and begin the payment of rent upon a total of not less than twenty thousand acres.

Upon written notice by the Lessee to the Government of Liberia of Lessee's intention to make a selection of land hereunder within a named territory Lessee shall have six (6) months thereafter to select land within such territory and upon the filing by Lessee with the Government within such six (6) months of written notice of the selection of land within such designated territory the title of such selected land shall vest in Lessee for the purpose named in this Agreement.

It is not intended hereby to deny Lessee the right to make selection of lands hereunder without such previous notification of intention to select within six (6) months; but if such last named notification is filed the same shall have the effect of preventing others from acquiring title within such territory during such six (6) months.

(c) As and when the Lessee takes possession of lands selected by it under this Agreement and yearly thereafter in advance, Lessee shall pay to the Government rent therefor (unless otherwise paid by special agreement) at the rate of six cents (6¢) per acre per annum in any coin or currency of the United States of America which at the time of payment is legal tender for public and private debts. As long as any of the bonds issued under the terms of the Loan Agreement of 1926, as amended, shall remain outstanding and unpaid, such rent payments shall be made to The National City Bank of New York at its office in New York City in the United States of America and receipted for by the said Bank on behalf of the Government.[9]

(d) Lessee shall pay to the Government a revenue tax equivalent to one per centum (1%) of the value of all rubber and other

[9] Amendment of December 28, 1939, Annex I.

commercial products of its plantations shipped from Liberia, calculated upon the closing prices of such products, or products of similar grade, prevailing on the New York market on the date of departure of the carrying vessel from a Liberian port, without deduction from such price of any costs or expenses whatsoever. The tax shall be payable in any United States currency which, at the time of payment, shall be legal tender for the payment of debts. Payments shall be made semi-annually on the first day of April and the first day of October in each calendar year, and each payment shall include the tax payable upon all shipments of rubber and other products of the plantations which have been shipped from Liberia in the preceding period of six months ending two months before each of the semi-annual payment dates. The tax shall be paid to the National City Bank of New York and receipted for by said Bank on behalf of the Government.[10]

(e) Any taxes which may become payable by virtue of the laws of the Republic by any person or persons carried on the payroll of the Lessee, if the Lessee so desires, shall be collected as follows: The Lessee may come to an arrangement with the Treasury Department of the Republic of Liberia which shall regulate the method of collection and payment of such taxes. But the Lessee shall in no event be held to collect in any year the tax for a greater number of employees than the average employed during the year.

The Lessee's employees and labourers engaged in work on its plantations shall, while so employed, be exempt from the performance of personal labour upon the public roads, to which they might otherwise be subject; and furthermore, all such employees and labourers in the service of the Lessee shall be permitted to perform such service for military training as may be required of them in time of peace upon land to be provided by the Government contiguous to the plantations upon which they are respectively employed.[11]

(f) Should the rent reserved on any piece or parcel of ground selected by the Lessee be behind or unpaid on any day of payment whereon the same ought to be paid as herein provided, or if default should be made in any of the covenants hereinbefore contained on the part of Lessee to be paid, kept and performed, and if such default in the payment of rent or otherwise shall

[10] Amendment of December 28, 1939, Annex I.
[11] Amendment of November 10, 1937, Annex G.

continue after six months written notice of the existence of such default served by the Government upon the Lessee, then it shall be lawful for the Government to cancel this lease as to that piece or parcel of ground, the rent for which is in default or in respect of which piece or parcel any other default exists as specified in such notice, and to reenter into and upon the said demised premises and to again repossess and enjoy the same. But if the Lessee shall, within said period of six (6) months after written notice as aforesaid, make good the default complained of in said notice, no right of cancellation shall thereafter exist because of such default. The notice required by this paragraph to be served on the Lessee shall be delivered to the representative of the Lessee in the Republic of Liberia and a duplicate thereof shall be simultaneously sent by registered mail to the President of the Lessee at its head office in the City of Akron, State of Ohio, United States of America. The Lessee shall promptly notify the Government of any change in the location of its head office and thereafter any such notice shall be addressed accordingly.

ARTICLE IV

It is further agreed between the parties hereto as follows:

(a) The Lessee will not import unskilled foreign labour for the carrying out of any operation or development undertaken by virtue of this or any other grant except in the event the local labour supply should prove inadequate to the Lessee's needs. In the event that the local labour supply should prove inadequate as aforesaid Lessee undertakes to import only such foreign unskilled labour as shall be acceptable to the Government of Liberia. It is understood and agreed that Lessee shall not have in its employ in Liberia more than 1500 white employees at any one time.

(b) Should the operations of the Lessee under this Agreement cease for a period of three consecutive years then all and singular of the rights of the Lessee hereunder shall become extinguished and void and this Agreement shall become of no effect but such cancellation of this Agreement shall not affect any rights granted by the Government to the Lessee under any other Agreement.

(c) The rights by this Agreement granted to the Lessee shall not be sold, transferred or otherwise assigned by the Lessee to any person, firm, group or trust without the written consent thereto of the Liberian Government previously had and obtained.

(d) The Government reserves the right to construct roads, highways, railroads, telegraph and telephone lines and other lines of communication through any and all plantations owned and operated by Lessee; but the Government shall pay to Lessee all damage which will be caused to Lessee's property by the construction and operation of such roads or other lines of communication; such damage to be ascertained in accordance with the general law of the Republic of Liberia.

(e) The Lessee shall have the right to develop for its own use such natural water power and hydroelectric power as may be capable of development upon any of the tracts of land selected by the Lessee under this Agreement and Lessee shall have the right to construct and maintain power lines over any Government lands in order to convey power so developed from one tract of land selected by Lessee to any other tract.

(f) Tribal reserves of lands set aside for the communal use of any tribe within the Republic of Liberia are excluded from the operation of this Agreement. Should any question arise as to the limits and extent of such reserves such question shall be finally determined by the Secretary of Interior of Liberia on a reference by the Lessee.

(g) Railroads and canals constructed and established by Lessee outside the confines of the Lessee's tracts selected hereunder shall during the life of this Agreement be exempted from all taxation so long as they be used only for the purposes of the operations of Lessee upon lands held under this Agreement. In the event that such lines of communication shall be used by Lessee for general commercial purposes to serve others for hire then while so used they shall be subject to taxation under the general laws of Liberia.[12]

(h) It is further agreed that at the expiration of the term of this lease hereinabove provided or of any extension thereof or upon the cancellation of this Agreement at any earlier time such buildings and improvements erected by the Lessee upon the land selected hereunder as shall not have been removed before the expiration or cancellation of the lease shall become the property of the Government of Liberia without charge or condition.

(i) It is further agreed that if hereafter the Government shall grant to any other person, firm or corporation any rights in connection with the production of rubber in Liberia upon more favourable terms and conditions in any respect than those

[12] Amendment of March 20, 1935, Annex B.

granted in this Agreement such more favourable terms and conditions shall inure to the benefit of the Lessee herein the same as if such more favourable terms and conditions were incorporated herein.

(j) It is further agreed that the Lessee shall use its best efforts to secure either from the Government of the United States or with the approval of the Secretary of State of the United States from some other person or persons a loan of not less than five million dollars to establish a credit for public developments in the Republic of Liberia to the end that the credit may be a revolving credit set up through reserves so as to meet the future requirement of funds for such developments. Such loan shall be upon terms and conditions to be negotiated by a Commission appointed by the President of Liberia who shall proceed promptly to the United States for this purpose. It is understood that such terms and conditions as may be agreed upon shall be subject to the approval of the Legislature of the Republic of Liberia.

(k) Wherever in this Agreement the Government grants to the Lessee the right to build and operate a railroad or to use the highways and waterways, it is understood that the Lessee is not seeking and is not granted public utility or common carrier privileges and that the same are not intended to be conveyed to it.

(l) The Lessee shall be entitled to establish, maintain and operate an aerial transportation system and necessary landing facilities therefor upon the lands selected and held under this Agreement and beyond the confines thereof; provided, however, that in the event that Lessee shall make use of Government land for the establishment of landing fields rent shall be paid therefor in accordance with paragraph (c) of Article III hereof. In the event that such lines of aerial transportation shall be used by Lessee for general commercial purposes to serve others for hire, then while so used they shall be subject to taxation under the general laws of Liberia.[14]

(m) During the life of this Agreement the Lessee shall at all times have access to the port and harbour facilities at Monrovia, or in any other district of the Republic where it may be carrying on operations, upon not less favourable terms than is accorded others under existing treaties and the laws of the Re-

[13] Amendment of March 20, 1935, Annex B.
[14] Amendment of March 20, 1935, Annex B.

public of Liberia. It shall be privileged to lease available lands in all ports of entry from the Government upon favourable terms.

(n) All or any questions in dispute arising out of this Agreement between the Government and the Lessee which cannot be harmonized or adjusted by the Lessee and the Government shall be referred to the Liberian Supreme Court or any one of the Justices thereof for arbitration on application of either party; and said Court shall make appointment of three arbitrators (one of whom shall be nominated for such purpose to said Court by the President of Liberia, and one of whom shall be nominated for such purpose to said Court by the representative of the Lessee in charge of Lessee's affairs in the Republic of Liberia, the third arbitrator being the Court's selection without nomination) to hear and determine such dispute within five days after application being filed, upon first being satisfied of the service of notice of such application at least five days previous to the filing of the application (a) by delivery of a copy of the application to the Attorney General of Liberia, or, in his absence, to the officer in charge of his office when said application is made by the Lessee, and (b) by delivery of a copy of the application to the representative of the Lessee in charge of Lessee's affairs in the Republic of Liberia and (c) by mailing a duplicate thereof on the same date by registered mail to the President of the Lessee at its head office in the City of Akron, State of Ohio, United States of America, when said application is made by the Government;

That the arbitrators so appointed as aforesaid shall render their decision of the question or questions in dispute in writing and file same with the Clerk of the Supreme Court, together with copy of testimony taken and statement of proceedings had within fifteen days after their appointment as aforesaid. Unless an application for further arbitration, as hereinafter provided, be made by either party within a period of four months after said decision is given, said decision shall be a definitive settlement of the question or questions in dispute and shall be binding upon both parties, their Agents or Assigns, and the Government of Liberia agrees to make said decision operative. Should, however, either party feel aggrieved at the decision of the Arbitrators then the Government agrees to arrange with the United States Department of State for a further arbitration of the question or questions submitted by either or both parties; provided, however, that in the case of such further arbitration each party shall bear its own respective costs; and provided further that the procedure for such further arbitration shall be as follows:

Written notice of desire for further arbitration shall be given by either party to the other within four months after the written decision of the arbitrators in the first instance has been filed with the Clerk of the Supreme Court; thereupon both parties shall prepare and file with the Clerk of the Supreme Court within sixty days after service of the notice written statements of the questions in dispute, and these statements together with a copy of the testimony and proceedings of the arbitrators together with a copy of their decision, shall be certified by the Clerk of the Supreme Court and delivered within five days after receipt of said papers in his office to the Secretary of State of Liberia who will thereupon promptly arrange with the United States Department of State for further arbitration of the questions in dispute, the decision of which arbitration shall be final and binding upon both parties to this Agreement.

It is understood and agreed that the final decision shall become effective thirty days after such final decision has been rendered and shall not be retroactive. It is also understood and agreed that during the period of arbitration, the Lessee shall be permitted by the Government to carry on without interference, all operations under this Agreement, including the operations involved in the subject matter of dispute, which the Lessee had undertaken, and, being undertaken, had not been objected to by the Government prior to the dispute arising. It is understood, however, that the fact there was no objection on the part of the Government shall not prejudice its rights in the subject matter of dispute.

It is hereby expressly understood and agreed that the arbitration procedure provided for herein does not apply to civil or criminal proceedings to be brought by or against employees of the Lessee in Liberia.

Appendix 6

THE LOAN AGREEMENT OF 1926

Between Liberia and Finance Corporation of America, as permanently amended

Article I

The Government covenants with the Corporation that it will cause to be sanctioned, created and issued its "External Forty Year Sinking Fund Seven Per Cent. Gold Bonds" (hereinafter referred to as the "Bonds") in the aggregate principal amount of five million dollars ($5,000,000), gold coin of the United States of America, to be dated as of January first, 1926, to mature on January first, 1966, to bear interest from the date thereof at the rate of seven per cent (7%) per annum, payable semi-annually on July first and January first in each year, to be executed by the Secretary of the Treasury of the Government, or by such other officer of the Government as may be designated in writing to the Fiscal Agent by the President of the Government, to be imprinted with the seal of the Government or a facsimile thereof, and to have interest coupons attached, executed with the facsimile signature of its Secretary of the Treasury, and to be authenticated by the signature of the Fiscal Agent thereon indorsed, which Bonds, interest coupons and Fiscal Agent's Certificate are to be substantially in the forms hereto attached, marked Exhibit "A"; provided, nevertheless, that anything in this agreement or the amendments thereto to the contrary notwithstanding, or in the bonds and interest coupons issued under the provisions thereof, the obligation of the Government to pay the principal of and interest on the bonds shall be satisfied, on and after February 24th, 1936, by the payment of dollars in any coin or currency of the United States of America which at the time of payment is legal tender for the payment of public and private debts, and provided further, that from and after and including the first day of January, 1945, the rate of interest upon the said bonds shall be reduced from seven (7%) per cent per annum to five per cent per annum; and provided further, that for the period beginning with the first day of January, 1945, and continuing until the thirty-first day of December, 1949, the obligation of the Government to pay interest on the said bonds shall be satisfied by the payment of interest at the rate of four per cent per annum. Only such Bonds as shall be so authenticated shall be valid or obligatory for any purpose, and such authentication upon any outstanding Bond shall be conclusive evidence and the only competent evidence that such Bond is one of the Bonds of this loan. The Bonds shall be issued in the denomination of $500 or $1,000, as the Corporation may designate, and shall be registerable as to principal, but not as to interest.

The Government hereby appoints The National City Bank of New York as Fiscal Agent of the Government, with the duties and powers hereinafter set forth. The Fiscal Agent shall maintain at its Head Office in the Borough of Manhattan, City and State of New York, United States of America, a book or books in which shall be kept a record of Bonds registered as to principal, and it may establish such regulations with reference to the registration of Bonds as it may deem necessary or advisable; the cost of such registration to be paid, as and when stated to it, by the Government.

Article II

The Government covenants that both principal and interest of the Bonds will be paid promptly as they respectively become due, and that any and all sums and expenses in connection with the service of the issue will be paid in conformity with Article V hereof, and that payments shall be made in the Borough of Manhattan, City and State of New York, United States of America, at the head office of the Fiscal Agent, in gold coin of the United States of America of or equal to the present standard of weight and fineness and shall be paid, without deduction for or on account of any taxes, assessments or other governmental charges or duties now or hereafter levied or to be levied by or under the authority of the Government or any taxing authority thereof; provided, nevertheless, that on and after February 24, 1936, any and all obligations of the Government hereunder shall be satisfied by the payment of dollars in any coin or currency of the United States of America which at the time of payment is legal tender for public and private debts.

Article III

The Fiscal Agent shall be entitled to treat the person in whose name any Bond shall at the time be registered as to principal as the owner thereof for the purpose of receiving payment of such principal, and payment of or on account of the principal of any Bond which shall at the time be registered as to principal shall be made only to or upon the order of such registered owner. The bearer of any Bond which shall not at the time be registered as to principal, and the bearer of any interest coupon pertaining to any Bond (whether such Bond shall be registered as to principal or not) shall be deemed to be the absolute owner thereof for any and all purposes, and neither the Government nor the Fiscal Agent shall be affected by any notice to the contrary.

Article IV

In case any Bond, with interest coupons, shall be mutilated, destroyed or lost, the Government, in its discretion, may issue, and thereupon the Fiscal Agent shall authenticate and deliver, a new Bond of like series, denomination, tenor and date, in exchange and substitution for, and upon the cancellation of, the mutilated Bond and its interest coupons, or in lieu of and in substitution for the Bond and its interest coupons so destroyed or lost, upon receipt, in each case, of indemnity satisfactory to the Government and to the Fiscal Agent, and, in the case of the destruction or loss of any Bond or its interest coupons, upon the receipt, also, of evidence satisfactory to them of such destruction or loss.

Article V

For the payment of the interest on the outstanding Bonds and the amortization of the principal thereof at maturity, the Government will remit or cause to be remitted to the Fiscal Agent in the City of New York, United States of America, semi-annually on May first and November first in each year (so long as any of the Bonds remain outstanding and unpaid and there shall not have been deposited with the Fiscal Agent a sum in cash sufficient to pay, and for the purpose of paying same), an amount in cash sufficient to pay the interest to become due on all the Bonds then outstanding, on the next subsequent interest payment date; and, in addition thereto, on or prior to May first and November first in each year, while any of such Bonds shall remain outstanding and unpaid, a sum equivalent to, but not more than, one-half of the par value of the Bonds outstanding at each payment date divided by the number of years to run up to the maturity of the Loan, provided, nevertheless, that nothing herein contained shall be construed to limit or affect the provisions of Article XV of the Loan Agreement.

From the sums so remitted from time to time, the Fiscal Agent shall first set aside a sum sufficient to pay the interest on the outstanding Bonds on the next subsequent semi-annual interest date, and, after setting aside such sum, the Fiscal Agent shall apply the remaining sums so received, from time to time, as a Sinking Fund for the retirement of the Bonds, after January 1st, 1931, in the following manner:

The Fiscal Agent shall apply the monies in the Sinking Fund, as the same accrue and become available thereto, from time to time, to the purchase of Bonds in the open market (including, as well, any stock exchange) if obtainable with reasonable diligence at prices not exceeding 102 per cent of the principal amount thereof, and accrued interest.

Any monies in the Sinking Fund which shall not have been applied to the purchase of Bonds at least seventy days prior to the first day of October in each year shall be applied on such first day of October to the redemption of Bonds, by lot, at the redemption price of 102 per cent of the principal amount thereof, as follows: the Fiscal Agent shall select by lot an aggregate principal amount of such Bonds equal as nearly as may be to, but not exceeding, the monies then in the Sinking Fund, and shall thereupon give notice of redemption of the Bonds so selected, by publishing the same at least once a week for four consecutive weeks, in each of two newspapers of general circulation, published in the Borough of Manhattan, City and State of New York, United States of America, the first publication to be at least sixty days prior to the date designated for redemption, and by mailing a copy of such notice to each registered owner of such Bonds at his address appearing upon the bond registry books, on or before the date of the first publication of the notice. Such notice shall call upon the holders of the Bond mentioned therein to surrender the same, with all unmatured interest coupons attached, at the Head Office of the Fiscal Agent in the City of New York for redemption at the said redemption price on the date designated for such redemption. Notice of such redemption having been given as herein provided, the said Bonds shall, on the date designated in such notice, become due and payable, at the said Head Office of the Fiscal Agent, at the said redemption price, plus accrued interest, anything herein or in said Bonds contained to the contrary notwithstanding. After such redemption date, the Bonds designated for redemption shall cease to bear interest.

In the event bonds are retired through the operation of the amortization provisions of the Loan Agreement, as amended, between the date of deposit of the interest monies, and the date for the payment of such interest, the excess interest monies thereby resulting shall be held by the Fiscal Agent and credited against the next subsequent remittance for interest and such remittance shall be diminished by the amount so held by the Fiscal Agent.

Article VI

Any and all Bonds purchased or redeemed pursuant to any of the provisions of this Contract shall forthwith be cancelled by the Fiscal Agent and permanently retired and disposed of at the direction of the Government, and no further Bonds shall be issued in lieu thereof.

Article VII

The Government agrees that it will forthwith undertake negotiations with the present holders of the external and internal debt of the Republic for the adjustment of such debt and for the settlement of such claims as may be approved by the Financial Adviser hereinafter referred to, and that the Bonds herein provided to be issued by the Government and hereinafter termed "The Loan" shall be charged as a first lien,

On all customs duties of the Republic receivable on and after the date of the execution and delivery of this Agreement by the Government, whether in respect of imports or exports, and

On all of the revenues receivable on or after said date from head monies, and

On the land rent and the revenue tax on the products of the Firestone Plantations accruing semi-annually pursuant to the provisions of Paragraphs (c) and (d) respectively of Article III of the contract of October 2, 1926, as amended, generally known as the Planting Agreement, between the Government and Firestone Plantations Company.

The Government further agrees that, in the event that the above revenues should prove insufficient for the service of the loan, the Government shall first allocate from its other revenues such sums as shall be sufficient to make up the deficiency; provided, however, that so long as no more than One Million Five Hundred Thousand Dollars ($1,500,000) of the Bonds of the Loan shall be outstanding,

(a) In any calendar year when the sum of all revenues and receipts and the Reserve Fund of the Government shall be less than Five Hundred Sixty-five Thousand Dollars ($565,000), interest on the Loan due and payable for such calendar year shall be paid by the issuance and delivery to the Fiscal Agent within ninety (90) days of the ensuing year, of coupon Bonds for the amount of such interest or as nearly as the denomination of such Bonds will permit; and provided, further, that,

(b) In any calendar year when the sum of all revenues and receipts and the Reserve Fund of the Government shall exceed Five Hundred Sixty-five Thousand Dollars ($565,000) but shall be less than the amount required to liquidate fully the interest on the Loan, due and payable for such calendar year, the amount which shall constitute the difference between the sum of all revenues and receipts collected by the Government and the Reserve Fund for the said calendar year and said Five Hundred Sixty-five Thousand Dollars ($565,000) shall be paid in cash and the balance of said interest due and payable shall be paid by the issuance and delivery to the Fiscal Agent within the first ninety (90) days of the ensuing year of coupon Bonds for the amount of such balance of said interest or as nearly as the denomination of such Bonds will permit; and provided, further, that

(c) In the event that the sum of all revenues and receipts and the Reserve Fund of the Government shall exceed Five Hundred Sixty-five Thousand Dollars ($565,000) plus the amount necessary to liquidate fully the interest due for such calendar year, the over-plus shall be applied in the first place to the current normal amortization as required by Article V, as amended, computed upon all Bonds at the time outstanding; and provided, further, that

(d) In any calendar year in which the estimate of revenues and receipts for said year shall be Eight Hundred Fifty Thousand Dollars ($850,000) or more, but less than One Million Dollars ($1,000,000), the Government may appropriate for the purpose of the Basic Budget eighty-five per cent (85%) of such estimated revenues and receipts. In any calendar year when the estimate of revenues and receipts shall be One Million Dollars ($1,000,000) or more, the Government may appropriate for the purpose of the Basic Budget ninety per cent (90%) of such estimated revenues and receipts. All revenues and receipts, the total of which is in excess of the above percentages which are received by the Government shall be considered as Excess Revenues and shall be applied and expended as hereinafter set forth.

In the event that the total revenues and receipts of the Government shall in any calendar year exceed the amount required to be appropriated for the Basic Budget as provided herein, then at least ten per cent (10%) of such excess revenue, but not more than Thirty-five Thousand Dollars ($35,000), shall be applied to the payment of any arrearages of amortization then existing; at least twenty-three and one-third per cent (23 1/3%) of such excess but not more than Thirty-Five Thousand Dollars ($35,000) shall be applied to the liquidation of the principal only of the Government's floating debt incurred prior to the thirty-first day of December, 1934, and which was determined to be Six Hundred Fifty Thousand Dollars ($650,000) as of that date; at least thirty-three and one-third per cent (33 1/3%) of such excess but not more than the sum of Fifty Thousand Dollars ($50,000) shall be applied to the cost of labor, tools, and materials for the extention of the public roads; the remaining thirty-three and one-third per cent (33 1/3%) of such excess but not more than Fifty Thousand Dollars ($50,000) shall be carried into a Reserve Fund and used as hereinafter provided; the remainder of such excess shall be available for appropriation for the general purposes of the Government.

In the event the arrears of amortization are completely paid before the liquidation of the floating debt has been accomplished, then thirty-three and one-third per cent (33 1/3%) of the total excess revenue as defined therein shall be applied to the payment of the floating debt.

In the event the floating debt is completely paid, then thirty-three and one-third per cent (33 1/3%) of the total excess revenue as defined herein shall be applied to the extension of the educational and sanitation facilities of the Republic.

No excess revenue shall be expended during the calendar year in which it has been collected.

Coupon Bonds which have been issued for payment of overdue interest pursuant to the provisions set out herein shall be redeemable at par on any interest date upon notice given in the manner provided in Article V, as amended, and all such interest Bonds hereafter issued shall be stamped with a notice to that effect and shall bear interest coupons beginning with coupons maturing the first day of January or the first day of July, whichever the case may be, following the maturity date of the coupons, in payment of which the Bonds were issued. Any difference between the amount of such interest Bonds so issued and the amount of interest due, shall be paid in cash.

When payments are made to the Fiscal Agent on account of amortization of arrears, the Fiscal Agent may apply such funds to the retirement of Bonds notwithstanding the fact that no funds or insufficient funds have been deposited with the Fiscal Agent to pay the next subsequent interest or amortization installment.

Import and export duties of every kind and character whatsoever, head monies and all other taxes, imposts and revenues of the Republic, except the land rent and revenue tax on products of the plantations accruing semi-annually pursuant to the provisions of Paragraphs (c) and (d) respectively of Article III of the contract of October 2, 1926, as amended, generally known as the Planting Agreement, between the Government and Firestone Plantations Company, shall be collected through the custom postal and internal revenue administration, to be maintained by the Government under the supervision and direction of the Financial Adviser and certain assistants appointed as hereinafter stipulated who shall co-operate with the Treasury, Postal and Interior Department officials in the manner hereinafter prescribed. Until such time as the debt created pursuant to the Loan Agreement and all interest thereon shall have been wholly satisfied and discharged, the excepted land rent and revenue tax on products of the plantation shall be paid directly by the Firestone Plantations Company from time to time as they accrue to the National City Bank of New York at its office in the City of New York, and receipted for by the said bank on behalf of the Government. Such payments shall be accepted by the said bank for deposit to the credit of the Government in a special account to be entitled "Special Interest and Amortization Accrual Account of the Government of the Republic of Liberia." Withdrawals from said account shall be made only upon the order of the said Government.

Withdrawals shall be made by the Government from said special account in the following order of priority:

1. To the payment to the Fiscal Agent on the dates provided in the Loan Agreement of 1926, as amended, of such an amount as will equal the interest due and payable on the next semi-

annual interest date on all outstanding Bonds issued under the said Loan Agreement as amended.

2. Thereafter for payment to the Fiscal Agent on the dates provided in the Loan Agreement of 1926, as amended, of such an amount as will equal the current normal amortization requirements and requirements for then existing arrearages of amortization, if any, of the said Loan Agreement as amended.

3. Thereafter for the payment of any other amount appropriated for the purposes of the Government under the provisions of the Loan Agreement of 1926, as amended.

In the event the amounts so received and deposited in the said bank to the credit of the Government shall not equal the interest and current amortization charges due and payable at the next semi-annual remittance day and requirements for then existing arrearages of amortization, if any, then the amount constituting the difference between the sum of the amounts so received and deposited and the sum required to meet said obligations shall be remitted according to the provisions of Article V of the Loan Agreement, as amended. The Government obligates itself to appoint from time to time during the entire life of the loan the fiscal officers required by the terms of this agreement, who, during the life of this agreement, shall supervise and direct the collection of the revenues of the Republic from whatsoever source they may arise, and the application of the assigned revenues thereof to the service of the loan, which shall be administered in accordance with the terms of this agreement under rules and regulations to be made and to become effective for the purpose of carrying out the terms and provisions hereof.

Article VIII

As an additional guarantee of the prompt payment of the loan and to ensure the efficient organization and functioning of the Liberian fiscal service, and the administration thereof, the Government covenants and agrees to appoint to its service a Financial Adviser, who shall be designated by the President of the United States of America to the President of the Republic of Liberia and, subject to his approval, appointed to the said office. The said Financial Adviser shall at all times be subject to removal by the President of the Republic of Liberia, upon the request of the United States.

Article IX

The organization of the Customs and internal revenue administration of the Republic shall be supervised by the following officers, who shall be nominated by the Financial Adviser to the President of the Republic of Liberia (the Financial Adviser having first reported the names of the officers nominated to the Secretary of State of the United States), and shall be by the President of the Republic of Liberia appointed and commissioned to the respective offices with duties as defined in this Instrument. These officers shall hold their appointment during good behavior but shall be subject to removal by the President of Liberia, for cause, or upon the withdrawal by the Financial Adviser, for sufficient cause stated, of his recommendation of such officer or officers.

The auditor shall be appointed by agreement between the Government and the Fiscal Agent, and the Assistant Auditor shall be appointed by the President of the Republic of Liberia, to serve during his pleasure.

The officers to be so designated shall be qualified as to education and as to previous experience in similar or analogous positions in foreign service; and the President of the Republic of Liberia, before commissioning them for service hereunder, shall have the right to require satisfactory proof of such qualifications, with the exception only of the Financial Adviser:

1. A Financial Adviser, who shall be designated and appointed as hereinbefore stated, at a salary of Ten Thousand Dollars ($10,000) per annum.
2. An Official, who shall be designated Supervisor of Revenues at a salary of Five Thousand Five Hundred Dollars ($5,500) per annum.
3. An Official, who shall be designated the Bonded Auditor and who shall be appointed by agreement between the President of the Republic of Liberia and the Fiscal Agent at a salary of Five Thousand Five Hundred Dollars ($5,500) per annum.
4. A Bonded Assistant Auditor, who shall be appointed by the President of the Republic of Liberia.

The salaries of the officials named in sub-paragraphs 1, 2 and 3 hereof shall be paid monthly in United States dollars in New York funds.

The office of Supervisor of Customs and the office of Supervisor of Internal Revenues are hereby abolished.

Wherever this Agreement or existing legislation shall provide for any duties or obligations to be performed by the Supervisor of Customs or the Supervisor of Internal Revenues, then those duties and obligations shall be performed by the Supervisor of Revenues.

The office of Bonded Assistant Auditor to be appointed by the President of Liberia and the Fiscal Agent is hereby abolished. Wherever this Agreement or existing legislation shall provide that any duties or obligations shall be performed by the Bonded Assistant Auditor appointed by the President of Liberia and the Fiscal Agent, then those duties and obligations shall be performed by the Bonded Assistant Auditor appointed solely by the President of Liberia.

The officers above mentioned shall perform such duties and employ such persons as may be defined by law or prescribed by the Government, with or upon the advice of the Financial Adviser, as provided in Article XII. Such officers in the performance of their duties shall be responsible to the Financial Adviser; provided, nevertheless, that the Auditor and Assistant Auditor shall not be subject to control in making decisions upon matters within their jurisdiction. The salaries of said officers, with the exception of the Financial Adviser, shall be fixed from time to time by agreement between the Financial Adviser and the Government, provided, however, that, in the event of substantial changes in money values, the salary of the Financial Adviser and the salaries of other officers may be from time to time increased or diminished by agreement between the Government and the Fiscal Agent.

In the absence or during disability of the bonded Auditor, the bonded Assistant Auditor shall act in his place and stead. The salary of the bonded Assistant Auditor is to be determined by the Budget appropriation as made from time to time.

Such salaries paid to the Financial Adviser and the fiscal officers to be appointed as above stated shall include all allowances of any kind or character whatsoever; provided, however, that said officials shall, in addition to such salaries, be furnished suitable quarters by the Government; should the quarters furnished not be desired, commutation in lieu thereof will be given for the actual expense of quarters not to exceed the sum of eight hundred dollars ($800) annually; shall be furnished suitable medical care and attendance; shall be reimbursed for their actual traveling expenses incurred by them on official duty; and shall receive traveling expenses from the point of departure in the United States at time of appointment or employment, to their post in Liberia and return to the United States on termination thereof; and not more often than once in two years, shall receive their actual traveling expenses by ordinary route to the United States and return.

The Financial Adviser and the officers appointed by virtue of the provisions of this agreement shall be entitled to receive reasonable leaves of absence, cumulative over not more than two years, at full pay.

The number of the employees of the Financial Adviser, the Fiscal Officers and the Fiscal Service shall be sufficient for the efficient collection, audit, disbursement and administration of the revenues of the Government. The personnel shall be appointed by the President of Liberia upon the nomination by the Financial Adviser of persons qualified to fill vacancies. The Financial Adviser shall select his nominees from the Civil Service lists of qualified persons, if such be available; otherwise his nominations may be made at large, upon such tests of fitness as he may deem advisable. Such personnel shall serve under the jurisdiction of the Financial Adviser, who shall bear in mind the desire of the Government for the proper training of Liberian citizens for positions of trust and responsibility. The duties of such personnel, in so far as they may not have been prescribed by law, shall be prescribed by such regulations in pursuance thereof as may be issued from time to time by the Financial Adviser. The property and supplies for the use of such officers and employees shall be under the jurisdiction of the Financial Adviser. The number of employees of the Financial Adviser, the Fiscal Officers, and the Fiscal Service shall not exceed the average number of employees during the year 1930 or the average number of employees for the three-year period next preceding, whichever be greater, except by agreement between the President of Liberia and the Financial Adviser.

Article X

1. The Corporation agrees to purchase from the Government and the Government agrees to sell, at the rate of $900 per bond of $1,000, together with interest accrued thereon from time to time, pursuant to the terms and provisions hereof, and in the manner hereinafter stated, such an amount of said Bonds as will provide funds to be used by the Government for the purpose stated in the preambles hereof, not to exceed, however, the total aggregate amount of $2,500,000 face value of said bonds.

2. Said Bonds shall be certified to by the Fiscal Agent for the purposes of identification, and from time to time delivered to the Corporation, or its nominee, as against payment therefor at

the rate above stated, to be credited by the Fiscal Agent, out of monies provided for that purpose by the Corporation, to the account of the Liberian Government in the City of New York. Said Bonds shall be so certified and delivered from time to time by the Fiscal Agent, at the request of the Secretary of the Treasury of the Government, with the written consent and approval of the Financial Adviser but not otherwise, and payment for said Bonds shall not be called for in excess of the following schedule, to wit:

3. During the calendar year 1927, not to exceed the total aggregate amount of $1,500,000 face value of said Bonds;

4. During the calendar year 1928, not to exceed the aggregate face amount of $500,000 of said Bonds;

5. During the calendar year 1929, not to exceed the aggregate face amount of $500,000 of said Bonds.

If the Government shall fail to call for the full amount of said bonds provided for any one year the uncalled balance thereof shall not be cumulative except with the Corporation's consent.

It is understood by the parties hereto that the Government may offer for sale, in such amount as it may decide, the Bonds covering the remaining $2,500,000 authorized under this Agreement, when the total annual amount of the assigned Customs duties and head monies has exceeded the sum of $800,000 for two consecutive years. Such additional bonds shall only be sold in the American financial market and to or through the Finance Corporation of America or other American financial concerns, bank or bankers, doing business in the United States of America, and the Finance Corporation of America shall be given the first opportunity to purchase such bonds.

Article XI

1. The Government hereby authorizes the redemption of all of its Bonds now issued and outstanding, commonly called the 5% Sinking Fund Gold Loan due July 1, 1952, under the agreement for Refunding Loan dated March 7, 1912, between the Republic of Liberia of the first part and Messrs. J. P. Morgan & Co., et al., of the second part. The redemption of said Bonds shall be promptly carried out by the Fiscal Agent for the account of the Government in such manner as it may deem to be to the best interests of the Government, pursuant to the terms and provisions of the indenture of March 7, 1912. For this purpose

the Fiscal Agent shall use the first proceeds which it may receive from the sale of bonds as hereinbefore provided.

2. The Government further authorizes the payment of all costs and expenses incident to the preparation of this Agreement, and the preparation and execution of said Bonds, including fees of the Corporation's counsel, which the Fiscal Agent is hereby authorized and directed to pay from the first proceeds of said Bonds, as aforesaid.

3. The remaining proceeds of said Bonds purchased by the Corporation shall be from time to time paid out by the Fiscal Agent for the account of the Government for the following purposes, in the following order of priority, to wit:

4. Thirty-five thousand dollars, or such less amount as shall be sufficient to enable the Government to repay the advances heretofore made to it by the Secretary of the Treasury of the United States under the Act of September 24, 1917, known as "Second Liberty Loan Act" as amended and supplemented, and the interest thereon;

5. Such amount as shall be certified by the Financial Adviser as being sufficient to enable the Government to pay its internal funded debt, and the interest thereon;

6. Such amount as shall be certified by the Financial Adviser as being sufficient to enable the Government to pay its internal floating debt;

7. Improvements and developments as set out in the preamble on page 1, sub-paragraphs (a), (b), (c), (d), (e) and (f).

Such payments shall be made from time to time by the Fiscal Agent from funds available in its hands therefor to the credit of the Government, upon the request of the Secretary of the Treasury of the Republic of Liberia, certified and approved in manner and form satisfactory to the Fiscal Agent by the Financial Adviser.

Article XII

1. The Government agrees that the Secretary of the Treasury, Secretary of the Interior, Secretary of War, Postmaster-General, and other officials shall co-operate with the Financial Adviser to bring order and system into the finances of the Government, and to that end the Financial Adviser shall devise for the Republic of Liberia and for any local governmental authority therein such methods of accounting, rules and regulations for the collection, and administration of the public revenues and receipts as may be necessary to assure the collection of such revenues and the en-

forcement of the laws, rules and regulations pertaining thereto; and such administrative orders or regulations having been approved by the President of Liberia (such approval, however, shall not be withheld provided said rules and regulations as provided for in this article are not contrary to law and apply to the collection and administration of the public revenues and receipts) shall be issued at the request of the Financial Adviser by the department head for whose department or under whose jurisdiction any such regulations, rule or order applies. The Government shall fix penalties not inconsistent with the constitution and laws of Liberia for the violation of such administrative order, rules and regulations as may be issued as above.

2. Only the Financial Adviser as such is authorized to communicate directly with any official or branch of the Government, but by agreement between the Government and the Financial Adviser, any official appointed under this Agreement may be authorized to correspond directly with any official of the Government with whom he may have business.

3. For the further security of the revenues and receipts, the Government shall maintain a Liberian Frontier Force, and shall further maintain patrol service by sea as may be necessary from time to time. The patrol service by sea shall be administered by the Customs Service. The Frontier Force shall be administered by the War Department. The strength of the Frontier Force shall be fixed by agreement between the President of Liberia and the Financial Adviser, and it shall not be increased or decreased in number without the agreement of the Financial Adviser, except temporarily in case of emergency declared to be such by the Government. A duly qualified and experienced officer of American nationality shall be employed for the Government by the President of Liberia who shall report directly to the President of Liberia and who shall be senior in rank to the commanding officer of said Frontier Force. The salary of said officer shall not exceed the sum of (U. S.) $5,000 per annum; provided, however, that said sum may be at any time increased or diminished by agreement between the Government and the Fiscal Agent. Such salary shall include all allowances except medical care and attendance, travel on duty and quarters suitable for his rank, or commutation therefor on the basis provided for officers in the United States Army drawing pay at the same rate, which shall be furnished by the Government. Among his duties shall be the preparation and execution of a plan of organization

of the Force which shall be based on the idea of creating an efficient constabulary organization for the purposes aforesaid, and which plan shall include the qualification and disciplining of all commissioned and noncommissioned officers and the training of the men in accordance with the best practice now obtaining in similar organizations.

4. The funds for the maintenance of the frontier force shall be administered by the Treasury Department under the same plan and system as for other sections of the Government.

5. The assigned revenues and receipts shall, during the term of said Bonds, be payable only in gold, or its equivalent, and the rates and the amounts thereof shall not be decreased without the approval of the Fiscal Agent, but may be increased by the Government so as to meet the expenses of the service of the loan, and the expenses of the administration of the Government. The Comptroller of the Treasury, together with the Auditor, shall prepare for the Secretary of the Treasury, the Fiscal Agent and the Financial Adviser, quarterly and annually reports of the financial administration and of the collection and application of all revenues and receipts.

Such reports shall contain the details of all financial transactions of the Government, and copies thereof shall be sent to the corporation.

6. The Government covenants to install and maintain the pre-audit system, whereby all accounts of the Government before payment shall be duly presented to the Auditor and shall be audited. The Auditor, upon the submission of any account for his check and after examination of the appropriation to which it is chargeable to ascertain that the same has not been over expended and that the account is correct, properly verified and payable, shall indicate his approval by appropriate signature and shall approve the transfer from the general deposit account in the designated depositary to the disbursement account in the designated depositary of a sum sufficient to meet the Secretary of the Treasury's check for the particular account and payee specified. The auditor shall only refuse his approval of an order of transfer in case of:

(a) Non-appropriation;
(b) Over expenditure of appropriation;
(c) Incorrectness or irregularity of the account to be paid;
(d) Lack of approval by proper official or officials;
(e) Fraud.

The decisions of the Auditor in relation to the approval or disapproval of accounts shall be final and conclusive, subject only to an appeal by the Government or the creditor to the Financial Adviser, which appeal shall be taken within ten days after notice of the ruling. The decisions of the Financial Adviser upon such appeals shall be final and conclusive upon the Executive but not upon the Judicial Branch of the Government.

No payments shall be made except under warrant of the President in accordance with the budget or appropriation law, and all payments shall be made by check on the disbursement account to be opened and maintained in the designated depositary of the general Government. Payments to troops or other payments which must be made in cash shall be by check to a bonded paymaster, who shall make the detail of disbursements in accordance with the audit rules and regulations which are to be prepared and enforced in accordance with the provisions hereinbefore stated.

7. The proceedings of the Legislature of Liberia relating to financial matters shall be reported stenographically daily by the Government, and typewritten copies of such proceedings shall be furnished to the President of the Republic, the Heads of Departments, and the Financial Adviser.

8. The Government shall annually enact a budget which shall set out in detail the estimates of all revenues and receipts for the calendar year and the details of all appropriations for expenditures chargeable in any manner against such revenues and receipts. The proposed expenditures shall be limited to three categories as follows:

Item 1. The costs and expenses of collection of revenues and receipts and the expenses of the various departments of the Government which shall include all General Administrative expenses, public works and improvements, national defense, salaries, allowances and expenses of the Fiscal Officers, the Military Adviser, and all other amounts which the Government is required or obligated to pay by contract, by law, or by any commitments or undertakings which are chargeable against the estimated revenues and receipts for the ensuing calendar year, provided, nevertheless, that the amounts required to be paid for service of the Loan shall not be included in this item one.

Item 2. Interest on the Bonds issued under the Loan, due and payable for the ensuing calendar year as provided in Article V, as amended, and Article VII, as amended.

Item 3. Current amortization requirements of the Loan, due and payable for the ensuing calendar year as provided by Article V, as amended, and Article VII, as amended.

For convenience of reference the combined detail of the estimates of revenues and receipts and the combined detail of all appropriations for expenditures as hereinabove provided shall be referred to as the Basic Budget.

In any calendar year in which the total revenues and receipts of the Government shall be less than Eight Hundred Fifty Thousand Dollars ($850,000) but shall exceed the total requirements of the Basic Budget then the amount constituting the difference between the sum of the total revenues and receipts so received and collected and the total requirements of the Basic Budget shall be deemed excess revenue and shall be applied and expended as provided by Article VII hereof, as amended.

In any calendar year in which the total excess revenue shall exceed the amounts required for compliance with the provisions of Article VII hereof, as amended, then the amount constituting the difference between the total excess revenue and the amounts so required shall be available for appropriation for the general purposes of the Government.

In the determination of the amount of revenues and receipts available for appropriation in any calendar year, only the net amount of the income derived from the operation of the radio communication system which shall remain after allowance is made for payment to foreign companies and administrations of their respective portions of tolls collected in Liberia, shall be considered as revenue.

At least thirty days before the opening of each regular session of the Legislature of Liberia the Secretary of the Treasury shall prepare an itemized budget for the ensuing year, which shall contain statements in detail of the probable revenues and receipts of the Government for the ensuing fiscal year from all sources, and of all proposed expenditures chargeable in any manner against such revenues and receipts. This proposed budget shall be prepared in consultation with the Financial Adviser, whose duty it shall be to assure that the amounts proposed to be appropriated for expenditure shall not exceed the resources of the Government, as shown by careful examination and comparison of the revenue estimates, and who shall further examine the proposed budget to ascertain that all expenditures which are provided to be made by virtue of any of the provisions of this Agreement shall have been properly included in the proposed statement of expenditures. The Financial Adviser may only refuse to approve the budget when and if the disbursements which should be included therein as provided in this agreement or by obligation of law have not been properly included, or when and if the budget submitted by the Secretary of the Treasury exceeds the estimates of the revenues as prepared by the Supervisor of Revenues in conjunction with the Comptroller of the Treasury, under the supervision of the Financial Adviser. In the event of the failure of the Financial Adviser to approve the budget as prepared by the Secretary of the Treasury of Liberia, for any of the reasons above stated and defined, the budget of the previous year shall be operative in so far as it applies to the ordinary operating expenses of the Government and the expenditures provided to be made by virtue of any of the provisions of this Agreement, for the ensuing fiscal year only. Within 10 days after the enactment of the budget, the Secretary of the Treasury of Liberia shall deliver to the Financial Adviser a copy thereof as enacted and a statement of all appropriations, regular and special, which shall have been made. No special appropriation shall be passed by the Legislature except in accordance with a supplement to the annual budget prepared and approved as herein provided with respect to such annual budget. All accounts of the Government shall be subject to examination and verification by the Financial Adviser at all reasonable times.

All revenues and receipts of the Government shall be deposited in a Bank designated jointly by the Fiscal Agent and the Government as the official depositary; and all deposits made with the said depositary and all payments made therefrom shall be in accordance with the provisions hereof; provided, nevertheless, that the payments of land rent and the revenue tax on the products of the Firestone Plantations made by Firestone Plantations Company to The National City Bank of New York for deposit to the credit of the Government in a Special Account, as provided in Article VII hereof, as amended, need not be placed in such depositary.

Article XIII

All the revenues and receipts of the Government except voluntary contributions to the Government in the form of gifts for a specific purpose shall be appropriated and applied as follows:

1. To the payment of all costs, expenses, commitments or obligations provided for in Item One of the Basic Budget as provided in Article XII hereof, as amended; provided nevertheless that in

no calendar year shall the appropriation for said Item One exceed the total amount of Five Hundred Sixty-Five Thousand Dollars ($565,000) except as provided in Article VII hereof, as amended.

2. Thereafter to the payment to the Fiscal Agent on the dates determined by Article V hereof, as amended, of an amount equal to the interest to be due and payable for the calendar year as provided in Item Two of the Basic Budget.

3. Thereafter to the payment to the Fiscal Agent on the dates herein provided, of an amount equal to the current amortization requirements of the Loan as provided by Article V hereof, as amended, and in Item Three of the Basic Budget. Provided, nevertheless, that the revenue derived from land rent and the revenue tax on the products of the Firestone Plantations payable semi-annually under the provisions of Paragraphs (c) and (d) respectively of Article III of the Planting Agreement of October 2, 1926, as amended, shall be paid directly by the Firestone Plantations Company to The National City Bank of New York which shall accept such payments without verification as to amounts and shall deposit the same to the credit of the Government in the "Special Interest and Amortization Account of the Government of the Republic of Liberia" for which provision is made in Article VII hereof, as amended, and promptly notify the Government of the amount of the payments so received. Said Bank shall pay the amounts so deposited upon the order of the Government as provided in Article VII hereof, as amended.

4. Thereafter according to the provisions of Article VII hereof, as amended, for the application of excess revenue.

5. Such sums as shall be set aside from time to time from excess revenue for the Reserve Fund shall be deposited in a Reserve Fund Account in the Government Depositary or by said Depositary for the account of the Government in a bank in the United States of America or Great Britain for the purpose of securing interest thereon, which bank shall be recommended by the Secretary of the Treasury and the Financial Adviser and approved by the President (anything in this Agreement to the contrary notwithstanding). The sums so set aside and deposited shall be conserved and applied as follows:

(a) So long as the total of all sums so set aside and accumulated in the Reserve Fund Account shall not exceed the amount of Seventy-Five Thousand Dollars ($75,000) in any calendar year, no transfer of funds shall be made therefrom except for the purpose of supplying sufficient funds for appropriation to the purposes of the Basic Budget, as required by Article XII, as amended, and Article XIII hereof, as amended.

(b) In any calendar year in which the funds so accumulated in the Reserve Fund Account shall equal or exceed the amount of Seventy-Five Thousand Dollars ($75,000) then and in that event the amount required in Article VII, as amended, to be carried into the Reserve Fund Account shall be available for appropriation for the general purposes of the Government.

The transfer of Funds from the Reserve Fund Account for the purposes of Paragraphs (a) and (b) hereof shall be done upon certification by the Financial Adviser of the amount available. Funds transferred for the purposes of Paragraph (b) shall be applied in accordance with a supplemental budget to be prepared by the Secretary of the Treasury and approved by the President. Such sums so transferred and applied shall be subject to the same audit and control as all other Government expenditures.

6. At the end of each calendar year, all unexpended balances of the budget or appropriations shall be reported, together with a notation of any commitments or reservations or amounts outstanding in suspense against the same, and the budget for the following year shall take into consideration any outstanding commitments or unadjusted balances, but no sums shall be expended after the close of the calendar year against the preceding year's budget, the purpose being that all expenses for each year shall be budgeted annually.

7. The Government shall make no expenditures, except as hereinbefore provided, and shall not incur any liability or obligation to make expenditures otherwise. All salaries and expenses incident to the collection, application and administration of the assigned revenues and receipts and the maintenance of the Frontier Force shall be disbursed in accordance with the provisions of this Agreement.

8. The Government, the Financial Adviser, or such person as he may designate, or the Auditor shall have the right at any time and from time to time to examine and audit the books and accounts of the depositary in connection with its acts as depository. Monthly or quarterly statements of such accounts shall be rendered by the depositary to the Secretary of the Treasury, the Financial Adviser and to the Fiscal Agent.

9. Agencies or branches of the depositary shall be opened or established in the interior or on the coast of Liberia at such

places as shall be decided upon by mutual agreement between the Government and the depositary. The places at which agencies or branches of the depositary shall be opened shall take into consideration the requirements for the protection of the revenues and receipts of the Government as well as the convenience of their application and administration. Such agencies or branches of the depositary may be closed or withdrawn as conditions may justify and upon agreement between the Government and the depositary.

Article XIV

None of the provisions of the present Agreement shall be deemed or construed to create any trust or obligation in favor of any holder of any of the outstanding obligations of indebtedness of Liberia or in favor of any owner of any coupons or claim for interest on, or in respect of any thereof, or in favor of any holder of any claims against Liberia. Any and all claims against the Government which may not be discharged under the provisions of the present Agreement shall be submitted to a claims commission, composed of the Secretary of the Treasury of Liberia, the Auditor and the Financial Adviser. This claims commission shall have power to determine the validity of any and all such claims, and its decision shall be final.

Article XV

Until the Government has repaid the whole amount of the loan and all expenses incident to the services thereof, no floating debt shall be created and no loan for any purpose shall be made except with the written approval of the Financial Adviser provided that this is not to be understood as restricting the Secretary of the Treasury from arranging temporary banking credit for carrying out a budget approved as herein provided;

And provided further that the Government may negotiate with responsible bankers for a refunding loan at any time after 20 years from date of each issue of bonds, but before such refunding loan shall be accepted, the Finance Corporation of America shall have the option of taking the new loan on the same terms and conditions as such bankers may offer.

Article XVI

1. The Government of Liberia hereby agrees that the fiscal agency created by the Agreement of March 7th, 1912, shall lapse with the payment of the Bonds secured thereby, and shall

be in all respects superseded by the provisions of this Agreement.

2. The three separate agreements heretofore entered into by the Government with the Firestone Plantations Company, a Delaware corporation, providing for:

(1) Lease of the Mount Barclay Rubber Plantation,
(2) Lease of certain lands of the Government for the purposes of planting and growing rubber thereon,
(3) Improvements to the harbors of the Government,

and respectively containing immunity in respect of the payment of taxes and duties as therein stated, are hereby in all respects ratified, approved and confirmed, and it is understood and agreed between the parties hereto that this agreement is entered into in all respects subject to the provisions of said agreements between the Government and the Firestone Plantations Company, in so far as the same relate to the payment of taxes and duties on the part of it, the said Firestone Plantations Company.

Article XVII

The Government shall enact all such legislation as may be required for the complete authorization and legalization of the present Agreement and of all action called for by the present Agreement on the part of the Government or necessary or convenient to carry out the terms and provisions thereof.

Article XVIII

The Government covenants to designate as the depositary hereunder such bank in the city of Monrovia, in Liberia, as shall be agreeable to the Fiscal Agent, and such designation shall be terminated by the Government upon the request of the Fiscal Agent. Any arrangement which the Government may make with the depositary shall embody the provisions of this Agreement, and such depositary shall undertake to comply herewith. In case the depositary shall cease to act as such by reason of such termination of its designation or otherwise, a new depositary shall be designated in the same manner as above provided. Monies paid to the depositary for the account of the Government, as provided in this Agreement, shall be held by the depositary and paid out as follows:

Monies paid to the depositary under the provisions of Article XIII shall be deposited in one or more special deposit accounts, as may be from time to time determined necessary or desirable, and no expenditures shall be made therefrom. Transfer from these accounts of monies to be disbursed shall be on order of transfer requested by the Secretary of the Treasury and approved by the Auditor, in accordance with the provisions of Article XII, paragraph 6, and countersigned by the Financial Adviser, and such transfer shall be made only to a disbursement account to be opened and maintained by the designated depositary, on which disbursement account checks may be drawn for expenditure, as hereinafter provided. Such transfer orders shall be issued from time to time and shall authorize the official depositary to transfer amounts from a specific deposit account to the Disbursing Account of a sum sufficient to meet estimated disbursements to be paid by check of the Secretary of the Treasury. Supporting each transfer order the Secretary of the Treasury and the Auditor shall submit to the Financial Adviser a statement showing the amount of the previous transfer order, the amount necessary to cover the checks issued against the proposed transfer order, and the balance in the Disbursing Account; the statement shall likewise show the balance in each deposit account and the balance after the proposed transfer order is issued.

Monies paid to the depositary hereunder, whether remitted by the Fiscal Agent or deposited by the Treasury Department or any other officer or agency of the Government, shall be deposited in one or more deposit accounts to be opened and maintained by the depositary, and shall be transferred for disbursement to one or more disbursement accounts to be likewise opened and maintained by the depositary and shall not otherwise be expended or transferred. Such transfers from deposit account to disbursement account shall be made only as provided in the foregoing paragraph.

Monies in the disbursement account or accounts which are to be disbursed in accordance with the provisions of this Agreement shall be disbursed in the following manner—viz.:

(a) No sum shall be disbursed in amounts greater than those provided by the budget.

(b) Any unexpended credit in any account provided for in the budget may be transferred to any other account by agreement by the Secretary of the Treasury and the Financial Adviser and the approval of the President; provided, however, that transfers from the credit of a department or service to another department or service can be made only upon approval of the head of the department or service whose credit is being reduced and in case of withholding of approval of the head of the department or service the question shall be submitted together with the views of all officials concerned to the President whose decision shall be final. No budgetary transfers of unexpended credit shall be made from appropriations provided for by Items 2 and 3 of the Basic Budget as defined in Article XII hereof unless all interest and amortization for the current fiscal year have been paid in full nor shall any transfer be made from the appropriation for the Reserve Fund except as provided in Article XIII hereof or from the appropriation for the payment of arrears of amortization, road construction and arrears on the unsecured debt as provided in Article VII hereof.

(c) Should it be deemed necessary and desirable, monies available by reason of accumulated credits as provided for in Article XIII, paragraph 6, may be used, and an extraordinary or supplemental budget may be prepared for their disbursement, by and with the joint approval of the Secretary of the Treasury and the Financial Adviser and authorized by the executive power. Such monies shall be available for disbursement from the disbursement account or one of the disbursement accounts the same as other funds of the Government.

(d) All monies available for disbursement shall be expended only upon the submission to the auditor of a properly authorized and verified account showing the name or names of the person or persons to whom said monies are to be paid, and the article of the budget or appropriation law whereby such expenditure is authorized shall appear on the face of the request for payment, together with any other necessary information to enable the Auditor properly to examine and check the warrant for payment. Upon the Auditor duly examining and verifying the balance of the appropriation credit against which said voucher is to be paid, the Auditor shall signify his approval by an order of release from the designated deposit account to the designated disbursement account, of a sum sufficient to meet the check or checks to be made and drawn in payment of said warrant. Thereupon the Secretary of the Treasury shall sign the check and the auditor shall countersign to indicate his verification of the article of the appropriation law, the correctness of the charge, and the correctness of the check, whereupon said check may be paid by the designated depositary on presentation by the person to whom the same is drawn or by the specific person to whose order it has been transferred; provided, nevertheless, that funds paid directly by the Firestone Plantations Company to The National City Bank of New York, as provided in Article VII hereof, as amended, shall be paid by the said bank upon the order of the

Government as provided in said Article VII hereof, as amended, without compliance with the requirements of this article governing withdrawal of funds from the Depositary, but upon the order of the Secretary of the Treasury and Financial Adviser by virtue of official voucher and Executive Warrant.

(e) No checks shall be payable to bearer.

The Auditor shall prepare at the end of each month a statement to each departmental head and to the President and Financial Adviser, which shall show the condition of each article and detail of the current appropriations showing the amount appropriated, the amount expended to date, the amount reserved in suspense, if any, and the balance available for disbursement.

ARTICLE XIX

The Fiscal Agent accepts its appointment as such, and agrees to perform its obligations under this contract upon the terms and conditions herein set forth, including the following:

(a) If the Fiscal Agent shall at any time be in doubt as to its rights or obligations hereunder or with respect to the rights of any holder of any Bonds, the Fiscal Agent may advise with legal counsel, and anything done or suffered by it in good faith in accordance with the opinion of such counsel shall be conclusive in its favor as against any claim or demand by the Government or any holder of any Bond. If any dispute shall arise between the Fiscal Agent and the Government hereunder, the same shall be settled by arbitration as provided in Article XXV hereof.

(b) The Fiscal Agent shall not be responsible to the Government or to any holder of any Bond for any mistake or error of fact or law or for the exercise in good faith of its discretion or for anything which it may do or cause to be done in good faith in connection therewith, except only for its own wilful default.

(c) The appointment of the Fiscal Agent by the Government is irrevocable, except for good and sufficient cause; but the Fiscal Agent may resign at any time, by giving notice of resignation to the Government at least four weeks before such resignation takes effect, and by publishing such notice at least once a week for four consecutive weeks in each of two newspapers of general circulation, published in the City of New York, United States of America.

(d) In acting under this contract, the Fiscal Agent is solely the agent of the Government and does not enter into or assume any obligation or relationship of agency or trust for or with any of the holders of any Bond or its interest coupons.

Article XX

It is expressly understood, however, that all power and authority temporarily delegated under this agreement to the Financial Adviser or any officer appointed hereunder is granted solely for the purpose of facilitating the carrying out of this Agreement, and upon the discharge by the Government of the obligations herein assumed all said power and authority so delegated shall automatically revert unimpaired to the Government.

Article XXI

The Government shall pay to the Fiscal Agent reasonable compensation for all services rendered hereunder and a sum equivalent to one-quarter of one per cent of the face amount of all interest coupons, as paid, and to one-eighth of one per cent of the principal amount of all Bonds, as retired, whether paid at maturity or purchased or redeemed prior to maturity, as hereinbefore provided. Payment of such compensation shall be made to the Fiscal Agent in gold coin of the United States of America, in the City of New York, upon statements rendered semi-annually by the Fiscal Agent to the Government, as hereinafter provided. The Fiscal Agent shall allow and pay to the Government on monies other than deposits for the payment of coupons or the redemption of Bonds, remaining on deposit with the Fiscal Agent for thirty days, or more, interest at the rate of two per cent per annum. The Fiscal Agent may treat all such monies as time deposits. The Fiscal Agent shall not be answerable for the default or misconduct of any agent or attorney appointed by it in pursuance hereof if such agent or attorney shall have been selected with reasonable care, in which case the Fiscal Agent shall be reimbursed and indemnified by the Government against any liability or damage which it may sustain or incur in the premises, and the Fiscal Agent shall have a lien upon any monies deposited in the Sinking Fund preferential to that of the Bonds, for any such liability or damage.

Article XXII

The Fiscal Agent shall render to the Secretary of the Treasury of Liberia in each year semi-annual statements of account covering the semi-annual periods ending December 1 and June 1 in each year of all receipts and payments and expenses made or incurred by it during the respective periods, provided that the first statement shall be rendered for the period commencing with the date of this Contract and ending June 1, 1927. Unless objection to any such statement of account shall be made by the Secretary of the Treasury to the Fiscal Agent within two months after the receipt of such statement of account by him particularly specifying the ground or grounds of such objection or objections, the statement of account shall be deemed to be correct and conclusive between the Government and the Fiscal Agent. The Government shall promptly pay or cause to be paid, as part of the service of the Bonds, the expenses of the Fiscal Agent as shown in such statement. The expenses of such service may include, among other things, expenses of printing and advertising, cost of exchange and remittance of funds, brokerage charges, postage, cable, telegraph and telephone charges, charges of legal counsel and other usual expenditures.

Article XXIII

Nothing in this Contract expressed or implied is intended, or shall be construed, to give any person, other than the parties hereto, any right, remedy or claim or by reason of this Contract or any covenant, stipulation or condition herein contained.

Article XXIV

Notices to the Government in connection with this Contract, or the performance of any of the terms hereof, may be given by written communication, or by cable, addressed to the Secretary of the Treasury of the Republic of Liberia at Monrovia. Notices from the Government to the Fiscal Agent in connection with this Contract may be given by written communication, or by cable, addressed to The National City Bank of New York, at No. 55 Wall Street, New York City, United States of America.

Article XXV

In case of dispute between the Government and either of the other parties to this Contract, the matter shall be referred for determination to arbitrators, one of whom shall be appointed by each of the parties to the dispute; and, if such arbitrators shall be unable to agree among themselves, the Secretary of State of the United States of America shall be requested to appoint an additional arbitrator, who shall be of different nationality from the other two arbitrators. The decision of a majority of the arbitrators so appointed shall be binding and conclusive upon the parties to the dispute.

Article XXVI

The Bonds may, at the option of the corporation, be engraved in such form as to be eligible for listing on the New York Stock Exchange, and the Government agrees in such case to furnish such information as may be required in connection with any application to list such Bonds on the said Stock Exchange. The Government will pay, as a part of the expenses in connection with the service of the Bonds, the cost of such listing.

Article XXVII

The obligations of the Corporation under this Contract are expressly conditioned upon the due ratification and sanction of this Contract by the Legislature of the Republic of Liberia, and upon approval by counsel for the Corporation of the legality of the loan and the form and legality of the Bonds, including all proceedings in connection with the authorization, sanction and issue of the loan and the said Bonds; and the Government agrees to furnish to the Corporation prior to the delivery of any Bonds, all such documents, instruments, assurances and proof of legality as counsel for the Corporation and the Corporation may require. If the Legislature shall fail to ratify and sanction this Contract, or if the Government shall fail to deliver to the Corporation a temporary Bond within sixty (60) days after such ratification, or if counsel for the Corporation shall be unable to give their approval as above provided in this Article XXVII, then the Corporation and the Fiscal Agent shall be, respectively, relieved and discharged from any and all obligations or duties under this Contract, and the Government shall pay to the Corporation and Fiscal Agent, respectively, all expenses which they shall have paid or incurred respectively in connection herewith.

Article XXVIII

This Agreement shall come into force and effect when approved by the Legislature of the Republic of Liberia, and duly executed in behalf of the Government by the officer or officers thereunto duly authorized.